D

"BROTHER RAT"

"BROTHER RAT"

BY JOHN MONKS, JR.

AND

FRED R. FINKLEHOFFE

WITH AN INTRODUCTION

BY GEORGE ABBOTT

RANDOM HOUSE
NEW YORK

To our two most precious sweethearts, Emily
and Annabelle—whom we also call "Mom."

INTRODUCTION

BY GEORGE ABBOTT

As far as my observation goes, the theatre in Russia, Germany and America is far ahead of the rest of the world. The English, it is true, excel us in certain branches of acting—especially where beauty of speech is involved—and the French bravura school, as a thing of sheer technique, is hard to top. But neither of these countries shows the vitality and power in either writing or production that is to be found in the aforementioned. The Germans have had to march so much of late that their drama has been a bit neglected. But the Russians, despite considerable marching, still have a vital growing drama, and the Americans—who seem to have substituted sit-down strikes for marching—have progressed most of all. The Russians excel in all plays with whiskers. The Americans produce the best bare-faced drama.

There are no set rules for the bare-faced drama, and yet it has certain obvious characteristics. It has the characteristics of the people who create it. It is novel, brash, colloquial, fast and humorous. Our excellence in this particularly strident and vigorous kind of a play is the natural result of our desire to express that side of our natures. Obviously, there is a great variety to the form which this expression takes. *Seven Keys to Baldpate, Front Page, She Loves Me Not* and *Three Men on a Horse* are all different, but they are all inspired by the same American impulses and were produced with the same punctuation marks. Each season we find a great many of these extraordinarily energetic plays coming up to bat. Many of them are inept; most of them, perhaps. They are bare-faced enough but lacking in skill. But one thing is certain: when the hits of each year are numbered you will find conspicuous members of the bare-faced school among them.

"*Brother Rat*" is, of course, a member of the club in good standing. It is novel, not only in the rather different setting, but in its language. It is told with a slang so exclusively the property of its locale that if the words were used outside of their context, one would be at a loss for the meaning. Why, for instance, a blonde is a slow-ball, I do not know. But, I think that is the way they are going to be for me from now on. The authors of "*Brother Rat,*" moreover, have captured a quality of ingenious exuberance that makes the play even more American than the talk. And they have done that vital thing so necessary to good playwriting; they have made the talk and the action proceed and develop according to the logic of character.

The ability to characterize is the greatest gift that a playwright can have. Without it, all his fabrication, no matter how beautifully conceived, is tinkling brass. Without it, the actors are hollow and the suspense empty. The fact that John Monks and Freddie Finklehoffe have shown themselves to possess this gift in such a large measure is a promise that this their first play will be only one of a long series.

"BROTHER RAT"

Produced by George Abbott at the Biltmore Theatre, New York City, December 16, 1936, with the following cast:

(In Order of Appearance)

Mrs. Brooks	Curtis Burnley Railing
Joyce Winfree	Wyn Cahoon
Jenny	Anna Franklin
Claire Ramm	Mary Mason
Harley Harrington	Richard Clark
Bing Edwards	Eddie Albert
Billy Randolph	Frank Albertson
Kate Rice	Kathleen Fitz
Dan Crawford	Jose Ferrer
A. Furman Townsend, Jr.	Robert Foulk
"Newsreel" Scott	Gerard Lewis
"Tripod" Andrews	Robert Griffith
"Mistol" Bottome	Ezra Stone
Slim	David Hoffman
Lieutenant "Lace Drawers" Rogers	Vincent York
Colonel Ramm	Carroll Ashburn
Member of the Guard	James Monks
Member of the Guard	Walter Wagner
Member of the Guard	Robert O'Donovan

Directed by George Abbott
Settings designed by Cirker & Robbins

CHARACTERS

Mrs. Brooks

Joyce Winfree

Jenny

Claire Ramm

Harley Harrington

Bing Edwards

Billy Randolph

Kate Rice

Dan Crawford

"Tripod" Andrews

"Newsreel" Scott

A. Furman Townsend, Jr.

Grant Bottome

Lieutenant "Lace Drawers"
   Rogers

Slim

Colonel Ramm

Members of the Guard

Cadets

The action of the play takes place at the Virginia Military Institute in Lexington, Virginia.

ACT I

SCENE I. Porch of Mrs. Brooks' home adjoining the parade ground. A Friday afternoon in April.
SCENE II. Barracks Room. That night.

ACT II

SCENE I. The porch, about one hour later. The same night.
SCENE II. Barracks Room. The following afternoon.

ACT III

SCENE I. In front of barracks, two months later. Two nights before commencement, 10:30 P.M.
SCENE II. Barracks Room, about two hours later.
SCENE III. Barracks Room. The following night.

ACT ONE

ACT ONE

Scene I

The present. A Friday afternoon in April before parade.

Scene: *Porch of a Southern home in Lexington, Virginia, adjoining the parade grounds of the Virginia Military Institute. In the right section of back wall there is a curtained window. Slightly left of center in back wall is a door in two sections opening off stage. Up left there is a gate leading into a well-kept garden, which extends farther back stage and off left. Left of gate there is an opening leading to garden and parade ground off left. Shrubbery and a tall white pillar complete the left wall. In upper right wall is a door leading into the house. Another tall pillar extends from stage to ceiling in left center. There is a small wicker divan right of center facing audience at a forty-five-degree angle. Left center there is a wicker chaise-longue, facing audience. Against the back wall between door and window there is a wicker table. Books and magazines on table. Magazines on chaise-longue and divan. There is a small wicker chair down right of this pillar and a porch rocker.*

Mrs. Brooks, *an elderly Southern gentlewoman, with a fine sense of humor, well dressed and wearing glasses is half sitting, half reclining on rocker. She holds a book in her hands, her fingers inserted in the pages.*

There is sound of two girls' *voices off stage.*

JOYCE
(Off stage)

Just say hello and come on over.... We have a date, you know.

3

CLAIRE
(Off stage)

Be there as fast as I can...

JOYCE

Well—hurry—(*Bugle off stage blowing Guard Mount is heard.* JOYCE MINFREE, *an extremely attractive blonde, Southern prom-trotter,* 20 *years old, enters from gate carrying a leather hat box in one hand, a light coat thrown over one arm and, tucked under her other arm, a crushed felt hat. She is about to call out when she sees that* MRS. BROOKS *is dozing. Crosses to door, puts her hat box on floor, throws coat and hat on top of box, and crosses to* MRS. BROOKS, *calling loudly enough to awaken her*) Gram... (MRS. BROOKS *bolts suddenly, and lets out a startled gasp.* JOYCE *laughs lightly.* MRS. BROOKS *looks up and sees* JOYCE.)

MRS. BROOKS

Heavens name! Joyce!

JOYCE

Surprise you? (*Kisses and hugs* MRS. BROOKS, *then sits on chaise-longue facing her.*)

MRS. BROOKS

Lan' sakes, child... nearly... (*Book falls off* MRS. BROOKS' *lap.*)

JOYCE

Oh, I'm sorry.... (*Picks up book and returns it.*)

MRS. BROOKS

Scare a body out of her senses.... Is that a spot on your dress?

4

JOYCE

Oh, that's nothing, Gram. (*Kisses* MRS. BROOKS) I'm so thrilled to be here... (*Gives* MRS. BROOKS *another hug. Over-enthusiastic*) How's my one and only Gram? What's been happening in Lexington? How's Jenny? Have they made you mascot of the baseball team yet? Wait till you see my new evening gown, Gram, you'll positively roll over and die.... (*Still bubbling, she goes to table and removes her hat.*)

MRS. BROOKS

Goodness, Honey, you're blowing off steam like a calliope.

JOYCE
(*Turns to* MRS. BROOKS)
Did any of the boys call?

MRS. BROOKS

Uh, huh, Mr. Harrington called this morning and...

JOYCE

(*Goes back to chaise-longue and kneels facing* MRS. BROOKS)
Wait till you see him, Gram... he's the smoothest thing.... Wasn't it sweet of him to ask me down? I only met him at mid-winters.... He's a darling.... What did he say, Gram?

MRS. BROOKS

Wanted to know when you'd arrive. Did Claire Ramm come with you?

JOYCE

She'll be over soon. She just went over to say hello to her mother and father. Harley, Mr. Harrington, you know, is going to take us to parade.

5

MRS. BROOKS
And that Mr. Randolph called.

JOYCE
(*Pretending indifference*)
Oh—did he?—Crazy Billy.... What did he say?

MRS. BROOKS
I'm certainly glad you're not down here on his bid. The way that young man behaved...

JOYCE
Oh, Gram, haven't you forgotten that yet? (*She laughs, trying to smooth it over.*)

JENNY
(*Exuberantly, talking as she enters*)
Look what the Lord done left on our doorstep.... (JENNY *is* MRS. BROOKS' *colored maid and sole companion. She has been in the family for years.*)

JOYCE
Jenny! (JENNY *goes to* JOYCE—JOYCE *shakes both her hands*) You're getting better-looking every day.

JENNY
(*Good-naturedly*)
Oh, hush up child... y'all better conserve that honey for them keydet boys.... They'll be a powerful long line on this stoop before long.

MRS. BROOKS
Jenny, will you take Miss Joyce's bags up?

JENNY

Sure will.... (JOYCE *sits on chaise-longue*) I declare, Miss
Joyce, y'all gettin' to look more like Miss Laura than Miss
Laura does herself.   Soon as I found out they wuz fixin' to
have that big baseball game tomorrow, I just knowed you'd be
showin' up somewhere 'round here.... (*Backs up a step.*)

JOYCE

I didn't forget you, Jenny. When you hang up my things
you'll find a little present on the bottom of the hat box.

JENNY
(*Taking* JOYCE's *bag and hat*)

Bless you, child.... Y'all brighten up this house more than
all the sunbeams in Virginia ... and I ain't beginnin' to mention what you're gonna spread around the barracks over yon-
der.... (*Points and laughs*) Y'all make me feel good for no
good reason. (*Emits a high-pitched chuckle as she exits.* JOYCE
watches her off then turns to MRS. BROOKS.)

MRS. BROOKS

If you're expecting Mr. Harrington, wouldn't you like to go
in and tidy up?

JOYCE
(*Looking like a million dollars*)

I certainly would.... I'm just a mess. Excuse me, Gram, I'll
be back in a minute. (*She starts for door, then sees* CLAIRE *on
stoop*) Claire! (*Takes* CLAIRE *by the hand, escorting her
through gate*) Here you are.
   (CLAIRE RAMM *is the glass-wearing Phi Beta Kappa type—
not very attractive but extremely likable. She is the same age
as* JOYCE.)

7

CLAIRE

Joyce, I think it's grand.

JOYCE

I was just ... (*To* MRS. BROOKS) Gram, this is Claire—

MRS. BROOKS

(*Rises, smiling, and goes to* CLAIRE)

How do you do, Miss Ramm? Your father and mother must certainly be happy to see you.

CLAIRE

Not nearly as happy as I am to see them.

MRS. BROOKS

Well, Claire, what do you think of our little town?

CLAIRE

Oh, it's lovely. I was afraid it was going to be just another Army Post, but this is the nicest place Dad's been stationed yet.

MRS. BROOKS

Well, we're very glad to have him here. . . . The new Commandant is very popular. We were disappointed that you didn't come down for the mid-winter dances.

CLAIRE

I wanted to, but I was so busy working on my fellowship.

MRS. BROOKS

Yes, I've heard about that fellowship. The colonel's mighty proud of you. (*She sits on chaise-longue, facing girls.*)

8

CLAIRE

Well, I haven't won it yet. (*Looking about*) This is a darling house, Mrs. Brooks.

MRS. BROOKS

Yes, I like it, living right here on Officers Row... (*Boys' voices heard off left*) ... Always know what's going on.... The boys must be coming back from baseball practice.... (JOYCE *jumps up and goes to gate.*)

JOYCE

Harley must be with them.

CLAIRE
(*Looking off left*)

Which one?

MRS. BROOKS

He's good-looking, but a seven-inning pitcher. After that he blows up. (*Sits on divan.*)

CLAIRE

Say, don't they look nice?

JOYCE

That blond one is Bing Edwards. You know, I showed you his picture in the paper.

MRS. BROOKS

Oh, Joyce, ask Bing to stop by the porch for a minute. I have a message for him.

JOYCE

All right, Gram.

9

MRS. BROOKS

If Bing could only bat the way he can pitch!

CLAIRE

You're quite a fan, aren't you?

MRS. BROOKS

I haven't missed but four games in the last six years.

JOYCE
(*Calling*)
Bing...Bing Edwards...(*Off-stage voices fade.*)

CLAIRE

Then you'll surely be there tomorrow.

MRS. BROOKS

The Southern Conference championship? I'd like to see you keep me away.

CLAIRE

Do you think we'll win?

MRS. BROOKS

Why, of course.

JOYCE
(*Talking to him as he approaches*)
Bing...I'm just delighted to see you.
(BING, *a well-built, healthy-looking, naïve, Southern college athlete, about 22 years old, enters, dressed in baseball uniform. He is wearing leather moccasins, carries his spike shoes in one hand, and his glove under his arm. Removes his cap as he enters.*)

BING

Mighty glad to see you, Joyce.
(CLAIRE *goes behind divan.*)

JOYCE

I declare, you look just like Babe Ruth.

BING
(*Embarrassed*)

Aw...

JOYCE

Have you seen Harley Harrington?

BING

Yeah...he was at practice, but...I think...yeah...he left
early.

MRS. BROOKS

Good evening, Bing.

BING
(*Sees* MRS. BROOKS, *crosses to her*)

Evenin', Mrs. Brooks...missed you today.

MRS. BROOKS
(*Pleased*)

Did you?

BING

Yes'm.

MRS. BROOKS

How's the arm?

BING

Pretty good ... I reckon.

MRS. BROOKS

I've got a message for you. Kate phoned this afternoon.

BING

Kate?

JOYCE

I didn't know she was in town.

MRS. BROOKS

Yes, she's coming over here before parade.

JOYCE

That's grand.

MRS. BROOKS

So you just better drop over.

BING

Thank you, m'am.

JOYCE

I'm just dyin' to see her. (*Turns to* CLAIRE, *who is slightly embarrassed*) Oh, excuse me ... Claire ... this is Bing Edwards.

CLAIRE

How do you do?

BING

Mighty pleased to meet you.

12

JOYCE

Bing is one of the greatest athletes V.M.I. ever had.... Aren't you, Bing?

BING

(*Embarrassed*)

Aw...not so great.... Well...I reckon I better get back to barracks...if I'm goin' to make it before parade.

JOYCE

All right, Bing. But be sure and come back.

BING

Sure will...well...'Bye...'bye, Mrs. Brooks.

MRS. BROOKS

Good-bye, Bing.

BING

Mighty pleased to have met you, Miss...uh... (*Backs up toward gate.*)

JOYCE

(*Quickly*)

Adams.

BING

Adams....

MRS. BROOKS

Adams?

JOYCE

(*Looks quickly at* MRS. BROOKS, *then at* BING. *Rushing him off.*)
You better hurry, Bing.

13

BING

See y'all later.... (*Exits, calling off stage*) Hey, fellas, wait a minute.

JOYCE

(*Goes to chaise-longue*)

Isn't he a darling?

MRS. BROOKS

(*Looks at* CLAIRE, *then* JOYCE)

Aren't you having trouble with your roommate's name, Joyce?

JOYCE

No, Gram.

MRS. BROOKS

But Claire's name isn't Adams.

JOYCE

I know, but...

CLAIRE

(*Walks around divan to* MRS. BROOKS)

You see, Mrs. Brooks... Joyce thought... being as my father...

JOYCE

Yes, Gram, we've changed Claire's name.

MRS. BROOKS

Changed her name? (CLAIRE *nods, goes to* JOYCE.)

14

JOYCE

We don't want the boys to know who Claire really is.

MRS. BROOKS

And why not?

JOYCE

(*Taking a step toward* MRS. BROOKS, *trying to make her argument sound as convincing as possible*)

Well, we want Claire to have as many dates as possible and ...

MRS. BROOKS

Why, of course ...

JOYCE

If they find out she's the Commandant's daughter ... Well ...

MRS. BROOKS

Would that necessarily put Claire on their blacklist?

JOYCE

You know it would.

MRS. BROOKS

I'm sure these nice young men ...

JOYCE

Now, Gram, be sensible.... You know they'd be polite, but, my goodness, look what happened to Barbara Johnson when her father was Commandant. It was terrible. And poor Squeeky Hutchinson! Just because he danced with her twice they said he was toadying up.

15

MRS. BROOKS

Well, all right....

JOYCE
(*Kisses* MRS. BROOKS, *takes a quick look at* CLAIRE)
Well, I guess I'd better get out of this dress if I'm going to parade. (*Goes to door.*)

MRS. BROOKS

Oh, Joyce!

JOYCE

Yes?

MRS. BROOKS

Will you please tell Jenny I want her?

JOYCE

Yes, Gram. Make yourself at home, Claire. (*Exits.*)
(*From inside house*)
Oh, Jenny!
(CLAIRE *stands center, embarrassed, then crosses to chaise-longue and sits facing* MRS. BROOKS.)

MRS. BROOKS
(*Looks at* CLAIRE, *smiles*)
You know, Claire, many exciting things have happened on this porch in the past thirty-five years, but this is the first time I've ever been a party to a re-christening....Suppose your father should find out about this?

CLAIRE

Oh, he wouldn't mind.

MRS. BROOKS

If I were you, I don't think I'd tell him.

CLAIRE

No, m'am...I won't...

MRS. BROOKS

Well, I'm sure I won't. I don't think I better even know about it.

(JOYCE *enters.* CLAIRE *rises and crosses to her.*)

JOYCE

Come on up, Claire. I'll show you my room.

(JENNY *enters.*)

MRS. BROOKS

Have you finished inside, Jenny?

JENNY

Yes'm.

JOYCE

This is Jenny, Claire.

CLAIRE

How do you do, Jenny?

JENNY

How you feelin'?

(JOYCE *and* CLAIRE *disappear into the house.* JENNY *crosses to* MRS. BROOKS.)

MRS. BROOKS

Will you tidy up this porch some, Jenny? We're expecting visitors.

17

JENNY

Sure will.... (*Picks up magazine off chaise-longue.*) I declare, honey sure attracts them flies...

MRS BROOKS

All right, Jenny. Never mind. (*She exits.*)

JENNY

(JENNY *crosses to table, then to divan*) Yes'm... (*Laughs. Then to* MRS. BROOKS *who has gone into the house*) But from now on it's gonna take a heap of concentratin' for them boys to keep their minds on the marchin' formations. (JENNY *sees some one approaching, right. Calls into house*) Miz Brooks....

MRS. BROOKS

(*From inside the house*)

What is it, Jenny?

JENNY

(*Calls*)

Here comes the first man in the big parade. (HARLEY HARRINGTON *enters. He is about 21 years old, an athletic, well-built, self-centered, vain cadet officer. Wears fatigue uniform—gray trousers, blouse with Cadet Captain's chevrons on both sleeves, gray cap.* MRS. BROOKS *appears in doorway.*)

MRS. BROOKS

(*Sees* HARRINGTON)

Oh... how do you do?

HARRINGTON

I'm Harley Harrington. Has Joyce arrived?

18

MRS. BROOKS

Yes. She's gone up to dress. Won't you sit down?

HARRINGTON

Thank you. (*Goes to divan.*)

MRS. BROOKS
(*Sits on chaise-longue*)
Will you tell Joyce that Mr. Harrington is here?
(HARRINGTON *sits on divan.*)

JENNY

Yes'm. (*Scrutinizes* HARRINGTON, *then goes into the house.*)

HARRINGTON

Has Joyce been here long?

MRS. BROOKS

No, she came in on the Number Four. I don't think she expected you so soon.

HARRINGTON

I am a little early ... But ...

MRS. BROOKS
(*Very pleasantly*)
Oh, that's perfectly all right. I'm glad of the chance to meet you. I've watched you play quite often.

HARRINGTON
(*Knowing she has*)
Oh, have you?

MRS. BROOKS

Yes, indeed. Football, basketball, baseball. You're a good athlete, Mr. Harrington.

HARRINGTON

Thank you, m'am.

MRS. BROOKS

I've watched you and Bing Edwards for four years, and I can't for the life of me make up my mind which one of you is better.

HARRINGTON

Well ... Why are you so interested?

MRS. BROOKS

Because of the athletic award.

HARRINGTON

Oh ...

MRS. BROOKS

For the past six years I've picked the winner correctly, but this year I can't decide.

HARRINGTON

Well ... Mrs. Brooks ... of course one never knows what may happen in the next two months, but ... I think you're talking to the right man.

MRS. BROOKS

That's one of the encouraging things about the youth of America.

HARRINGTON

Thank you, m'am.

MRS. BROOKS

I suppose you're all excited about the game tomorrow.

HARRINGTON

Well, when you've been in as many as I have, you take them in your stride....

MRS. BROOKS

Oh, are you pitching tomorrow? I thought that Bing...

HARRINGTON

No, I'm afraid not...Not this game. (*Phone rings off stage*) Bing's a fine fellow but you can't keep throwing fast balls all afternoon. (*Phone rings again.*)

MRS. BROOKS
(*Calls*)

Jenny!

JENNY
(*Off stage*)

Yes'm. (*Phone rings and* MRS. BROOKS *rises.*)

HARRINGTON
(*Rises*)

I hope I'm not keeping you from something, Mrs. Brooks.

MRS. BROOKS

Oh, no, I'm rather enjoying this. Besides, there's a question I've been wanting to ask you, Mr. Harrington.

21

HARRINGTON

Yes, m'am?

MRS. BROOKS

You know that game you pitched against North Carolina?

HARRINGTON

(*Not wanting to remember*)

Uh...Uh...yes.

MRS. BROOKS

Remember the eighth inning?

HARRINGTON

(*The die-hard*)

Eighth inning?

MRS. BROOKS

Yes, just before Bing Edwards relieved you.... (JENNY *appears in doorway*.)

JENNY

Miz Brooks...

MRS. BROOKS

What is it, Jenny?

JENNY

Miz Rice calling on the phone, m'am.

MRS. BROOKS

Will you excuse me, please, Mr. Harrington?

22

HARRINGTON
(*Hoping to escape*)
Maybe it would be better if I dropped by later on....I...

MRS. BROOKS
Oh, don't go....I'll be right back.

HARRINGTON
Well...I have an errand to do...and...

MRS. BROOKS
Oh. (JENNY *goes into house.*)

HARRINGTON
Will you please tell Joyce I'll pick her up before parade?

MRS. BROOKS
Surely.

HARRINGTON
Thank you, m'am. (*Exits, a puzzled expression on his face.* MRS. BROOKS *goes into house, and is heard calling* JENNY, *who is heard calling* JOYCE. *Then there is the sound of* MRS. BROOKS *talking on the phone.*)

MRS. BROOKS
(*Off stage, at telephone*)
Hello, Emily....Yes, she just arrived....Is Kate there?...
When she comes in will you tell her I've delivered her message?
...Oh, I'd be delighted....Yes?...Robert Taylor....(*Laughs.* BOYS *start talking off stage as* MRS. BROOKS' *conversation fades*)
I wouldn't miss it for the world....All right, dear...about
eight-thirty...Good-bye...yes...Good-bye...Good-bye.

"BROTHER RAT"

(BING, *dressed in fatigue uniform, lieutenant chevrons on both sleeves, enters with* BILLY *from gate.* BILLY RANDOLPH *is about 22 years old, fairly tall, reasonably good-looking, a Northerner. He has a vibrant air about him and has an ingratiating manner.* BILLY *speaks when* MRS. BROOKS *mentions "Robert Taylor.")*

BILLY
(*As he and* BING *enter and cross to door*)

The doll was just gettin' ready to buy. Instead a beltin' right in there, I'd spent two hours regulatin' the sights...and in walks the old lady. (BING *knocks on door*) What a break.... The best pair of pins in the State of Virginia.... And stacked up like a brick.... (JENNY *appears in doorway*) Hello, there, Jenny...

JENNY
Hello, Mr. Randolph. I just knowed y'all'd be poppin' up 'round here 'fore long.

BING
Has Miss Rice gotten here yet?

JENNY
No, suh.... I ain't seen nuthin' of her.

BILLY
(*Looking around*)

Hey, Jenny... Come here a minute. (JENNY *takes a few cautious steps out from doorway to* BILLY) I thought you were my girl....

JENNY
(*High-pitched chuckle*)

Sho' nuff?

24

BILLY

You've sold me out to the Indians.

JENNY

How y'all mean?

BILLY

Thought you promised to tip me off as soon as Joyce got into town.... Wouldn't even have known it if Bing hadn't told me. (*Shakes head gravely*) Jenny, you've broken our contract.

JENNY

Lan' sakes, Mr. Randolph ... Y'all don't need ...

BILLY

You don't know anything about a fellow named Harrington, do you, Jenny?

JENNY

He's the one done invited her down.

BILLY

(*Foot on chaise-longue*)

Mm ... mm ... That's bad....

JENNY

Yes, suh.... Looks like he's the high rankin' man this trip.

BILLY

(*Sotto voce*)

How's my stock holdin' up?

JENNY

What y'all mean?

BILLY

You know, Jenny ... How am I ratin' these days?

JENNY

(*Backing up to door*)

Y'all ain't ratin' too high around here, Yankee boy....

BILLY

(*Takes a step toward her*)

What's the dope? (JENNY *glances at door*) Come on, Jenny.
Turn it out.

JENNY

Well, I don't know what y'all done done.... But I sure heard
Miz Brooks frownin' on you.... (*Sees* MRS. BROOKS *approaching
and ducks into doorway.* MRS. BROOKS *enters.* BING *and* BILLY
remove their caps.)

MRS. BROOKS

Hello, Bing. Kate's on her way over.

BING

That's fine. (MRS. BROOKS *looks coldly at* BILLY.)

BILLY

(*Jovially, beating her to the punch*)

How are you this bright afternoon, Mrs. Brooks?

MRS. BROOKS

(*Rather frigid*)

I'm very well, thank you, Mr. Randolph.... But I have an
old score to settle with you.

26

BILLY
(Too surprised)

With me, m'am?

MRS. BROOKS

With you, sir. *(Scolding)* For keeping my granddaughter out until three o'clock in the morning the last time she was here.

BILLY
(Bluffing)

Oh, Mrs. Brooks. You must be confusing me with some other cadet.

MRS. BROOKS

No, I'm not.... I know my cadets. *(Sits on divan.)*

BILLY
(Bluffing)

Oh ... Of course.... Now I know.... I'll tell you how it happened, Mrs. Brooks.... I distinctly remember looking at my wrist watch ... *(He demonstrates by looking at his watch, with his forearm parallel to the floor, and horizontal to his body)* ... and both the hands were on top of each other.... It was exactly twelve o'clock, midnight.... *(Glances at* MRS. BROOKS *to see if he is registering. He isn't)* A short time later I looked at my watch again ... and I happened to get it in this position ... *(He turns his wrist so that his fist points toward ceiling, forearm perpendicular to the ground)* ... and both the hands were still on top of each other ... *(Looks at* MRS. BROOKS*)* and I thought my watch had stopped ... *(Feigns surprise)* Come to find out, Mrs. Brooks ... it was a quarter after three. *(Turns to* MRS. BROOKS, *who doesn't go for it at all)* Never happened to me before. Joyce is here, isn't she, Mrs. Brooks? I'd like to see her if I may.... It's rather important.

MRS. BROOKS
(*Rises*)

I'll tell her you're here.... How's that chemistry of yours coming along, Bing?

BING

Well, m'am ... I'm just about holding up above water.

MRS. BROOKS
(*Moving toward door*)

Well, keep up in your marks. We don't want to see you on the bench. (*Exits.*)

BILLY
(*Looking after her*)

I don't like the way she acts. (BING *turns to* BILLY) Maybe she's the one that's been working on Joyce. You know, Bing ... This doll has me baffled.

BING

Who?

BILLY

Joyce.

BING

Baffled?

BILLY

Yeah. Why is she down here on Harrington's bid? Think she's playin' me cozy?

BING
(*Sits on divan*)

I don't know.

28

BILLY

(*Assumes pose*)

Listen, Bing. I'm going to tip you off to something about women. Right off the bat they know if you've got a yen for 'em. That's what's known as female intuition.... They've got it ... and a dog's got it. And if they get to like you, see ... they stay up nights figurin' out ways to keep you from knowing it....

BING

They do?

BILLY

Yeah.

BING

Well, what about it?

BILLY

This about it.... Here's Joyce ... the smoothest fourteen-carat number that ever hit the Shenandoah valley....

BING

Yeah ... nice girl....

BILLY

Down on my bid for the mid-winter hops, she was bendin' toward me like a bush in a blizzard. When she mounted the train, and said good-bye, I could see it in her eyes ... she had the love-bag screwed on so tight ... she was gaspin' for breath....

BING

Did she?

BILLY

And now, only two months later, that weasel, Harrington, has
her down ... and she accepts. (*Crosses to chaise-longue.*)

BING

Well, why didn't you ask her?

BILLY

(*Sits facing front*)
I did.... No dice.... She's playin' me cozy.

BING

(*Looks at watch*)
I wish Kate would get here.

BILLY

No hurry. First call hasn't blown yet.

BING

I know, but I've got to make a deposit in the bank. I sent a
check uptown to the dentist yesterday, and not a cent in the
bank to cover it.

BILLY

(*Rises, crosses to* BING)
Well, listen, Brother Rat ... Give me the dough and I'll de-
posit it for you.... If you bounce any checks in the Commandant's face you'll *never* pitch.

BING

(*Takes money from wallet in blouse*)
Would you? ... Thanks. My scholarship money. (*Gives him
money*) If it weren't that I had to meet Kate ...

BILLY

(*Putting money in inside hat band of cap*)

Fifty bucks! Certainly pays to be an amateur. (JOYCE *and*
CLAIRE *enter.*)

JOYCE

Hello Bing. Hello Billy. (BING *rises.*)

BILLY

(*Very eloquent*)

...And I turned my eyes toward heaven and saw an angel
standing there.... (*Runs to* JOYCE *and takes her hand*) How are
you, Joyce?

JOYCE

Grand.... And so happy to be back. Billy, I want you to
meet my clever roommate. Claire Adams, Billy Randolph.

BILLY

(*Shakes hands with* CLAIRE)

Hello.

CLAIRE

So you're the Billy Randolph I've heard so much ...

BILLY

(*Smiles politely*)

That's right. (*Turns to* JOYCE, *ignoring* CLAIRE) Listen, Joyce,
I haven't much time, so don't stand there and argue with me.

JOYCE

Why, Billy, you know I never argue with you. (BING *looks off
left.* CLAIRE *sits on arm of rocking chair.*)

BILLY

That's why I love you. Now answer yes or no to the following question: I've got a date with you tonight...Right? (*Without waiting for a reply*) Right.

JOYCE

But...

BING

Did Kate say when...

JOYCE

She's coming right over....I'm just dying to see her. (*To
group*) Won't you all sit down? (JOYCE *motions* CLAIRE *to sit
with her on chaise-longue.* JOYCE *and* CLAIRE *sit on chaise-longue.*
BING *on divan.*)

BILLY

(*Standing, looking at* JOYCE)

Now about tonight...

JOYCE

No, Billy, I'm not going to have you take the chance of getting into trouble.

BILLY

No trouble unless I get caught.

CLAIRE

And how do you keep from getting caught?

BILLY

Well, I go up to the fourth floor, a section exclusively re-
served for the housing of rats—otherwise known as new cadets

32

—and I bring one down to my room—pay him the signal honor of letting him sleep in a first-classman's bed—and impress upon him the importance of keeping his head under the cover. Then, when the O.C. comes into my room to make his midnight inspection, and shines his little flash-light upon my hay, he finds to his intense satisfaction that it is occupied.

CLAIRE

Who sleeps in the rat's hay?

BILLY

The O.C. never inspects the fourth floor. Rats are too scared to run the block.

CLAIRE

Lucky for you that first-classmen room on the first floor.

BILLY

That's what makes the military system what it is. You start at the top and work your way down.

CLAIRE

What happens if someone sees you?

BILLY

Well...I'm an intimate friend of the Commandant.

CLAIRE

Oh, how perfectly darling!

JOYCE
(*Changing the subject*)
Have you seen Harley Harrington?

BILLY

(*Too sincerely*)

Isn't that terrible about old Harley? (CLAIRE *and* JOYCE *know better; they just look at each other*) How about it, Bing? (BING *hasn't been paying much attention to the discussion. He is slightly startled.*)

BING

What's that?

BILLY

(*Facing front*)

Very sad.... It's contagious too. Very unusual for yellow fever to appear so far north.

JOYCE

Yes, I know, Billy, but he was here just a few minutes ago.

BILLY

(*Shaking his head*)

It's a small world.

CLAIRE

So it is.

BILLY

(*Running his finger around the inside of his collar*)

Warm, isn't it? Well (*Walks toward* JOYCE), I've got important business to take care of before parade.... So... why don't you walk over to barracks with me, Joyce, and you can ...

JOYCE

But what about Harley?

34

BILLY

Where is he?

JOYCE

I don't know. He...

BILLY

Claire can wait for him.... (*To* CLAIRE) You don't mind waiting for Harley Harrington, do you, Claire?

CLAIRE

No, I don't mind. I don't know him but...

BILLY

He's a great guy.... You'll like him. Bing will keep you company.... He's going to wait for Kate.

JOYCE

Well...

BILLY

(*To* BING)

If Harrington comes, introduce him to Claire. (*Pulls* JOYCE *to her feet.*)

JOYCE

(*Rises—*BING *rises*)

I can't very well...

BILLY

She doesn't mind. Bing will bring her over. *He* can't miss parade. (*Takes* JOYCE's *arm, ushers her toward gate*) Come on, Joyce ... We've got to step off....

35

JOYCE

But, Billy...

BILLY

(*Ushering her off*)

Shhhhhhhhh...You'll wake the baby....Now tonight, "when churchyards yawn, and Hell itself breathes out contagion to the world," get all shined up in your full dike, 'cause I'll... (*Exits with* JOYCE. *There is a moment's pause.* BING *sits on divan.*)

CLAIRE

(*Both she and* BING *act embarrassed*)

You know this is my first visit to V.M.I.

BING

(*Looking anxiously for* KATE)

Yes?

CLAIRE

I'm surprised how old you are.

BING

Oh, yes, we're quite old....Well...I mean...the same as college...I mean...if we last that long.

CLAIRE

There seems to be plenty of excitement.

BING

Yes, there is.... (*Looks off right.*)

CLAIRE

(*Noticing his anxiety*)

She's late, isn't she?

36

BING

What? ... Yes, she's late. (*Pause.*)

CLAIRE

V.M.I. has quite a reputation, hasn't it?

BING

Oh, yes.

CLAIRE

Did you know General Pershing once made a speech and called West Point the V.M.I. of the North?

BING

Yes, I think ...

CLAIRE

That's quite a compliment, isn't it?

BING

Guess it is. (*Pause.*)

CLAIRE

How did you happen to come here?

BING

Uh ... Oh, a coach in prep school got me an athletic scholarship.

CLAIRE

Where are you from?

BING

Paris ... Kentucky. (HARLEY HARRINGTON *enters with bouquet of flowers wrapped in tissue paper.* BING *rises.*)

37

HARRINGTON

Hello, Bing.

BING

Hello, Harley.... This is Claire.... Claire... I'm mighty sorry... I've forgotten your name.

CLAIRE

Adams.

BING

Adams... This is Harley Harrington.

HARRINGTON

How do you do? Will you kindly take these in to Joyce and tell her I'm here? (*Gives her flowers.*)

CLAIRE
(*Rises, takes flowers*)
Well... Joyce left with Mr. Randolph...

HARRINGTON

Oh... Is that so?

CLAIRE

Yes, she asked me to wait for you.... Just a minute, I'll be right back. (CLAIRE *exits into house.*)

HARRINGTON
(*When* CLAIRE *is out of sight, he turns to* BING)
What the hell's going on here, Bing?

BING
(*Weakly*)
Well... you were late, Harley... and Billy...

38

HARRINGTON

He better learn a few manners. I had a date to take Joyce to parade.

BING

(*Naïvely*)

Well...Joyce wants you to take her roommate.

HARRINGTON

Is *that* her roommate?

BING

Yes...she's clever...

HARRINGTON

Migawd.... (CLAIRE *enters.*)

CLAIRE

All right...

HARRINGTON

(*Being the gentleman*)

Ready to go?

CLAIRE

All ready. (KATE RICE *enters. She is a slightly built, pretty, small-town Southern girl about 20 years old. She seems over-wrought about something but is obviously making an attempt to conceal her feelings.*)

KATE

Oh...

39

BING

(*Crosses to* KATE. *Beams*)

'Lo, Kate.... (*Is about to kiss her, remembers others, shakes her hand.*)

KATE

How are you, Bing?

BING

Good...uh... (*Looks from* HARLEY *to* CLAIRE, *pointing from one to the other*) Harley...uh... (*Looks at* KATE, *indicates* CLAIRE) This is...uh...

CLAIRE

Claire Adams.

BING

Joyce's roommate.

KATE

Oh...mighty pleased to know you.

CLAIRE

(*Smiling*)

You're Kate Rice....Joyce has spoken of you.

KATE

How is Joyce?...Is she here?

BING

No, she went off to parade with...Have you met Harley Harrington?

40

KATE

Yes, I think we've met before.... (*Bugle is heard off left, first call for parade.*)

HARRINGTON

How do you do? (*Turns to* CLAIRE) Sorry to rush you, but there's first call.... I have to get into a sash. (*To* BING) Coming, Edwards?

BING

No, I'll stay a bit....

HARRINGTON

Well, you know best....

CLAIRE

'Bye, Bing. I'll be rooting for you tomorrow.

BING

Thanks....

CLAIRE
(*Calling back to* KATE)

Good-bye....

KATE

'Bye....

BING

'Bye....

HARRINGTON
(*As he exits with* CLAIRE)

I can't understand Joyce.... (BING *watches* CLAIRE *and* HAR-

RINGTON *until they are well off, and then turns to* KATE *and smiles.*)

BING

How are you, honey? I mean...I'm glad to see you...I mean... (*He comes out of his awkward state, wraps his arms about* KATE *and kisses her fondly.*)

KATE

Sorry I was late, Bing....

BING

Sure is good to see you, Kate.... (*Picks her up and swings her around, beaming*) How you been gettin' along?

KATE

All right.... (*Gives him a fond hug.*)

BING

Must be great to be home again....

KATE
(*Holding up*)

Yes.

BING

How long you gonna stay?

KATE

Well, Bing... (BING *holds her in his arms.*)

BING

Gosh, Kate, you're pretty.

42

"BROTHER RAT"

KATE

Am I, Bing?

BING

Powerful pretty.... Never forget the first time I saw you standin' in the drug store...four years ago.... Made me feel as if there was a kettle full of hot water boiling up inside of me.

KATE

(*Looking up slowly*)

Thank you, Bing.

BING

I sure have been miserable since you went away to Roanoke. ...But it's nice to have you back. Remember last fall? Do you reckon we'll ever have that much fun again? (KATE *kisses him on the tip of his nose.*)

KATE

Oh, Bing... (MRS. BROOKS *enters.*)

MRS. BROOKS

Oh, my.... (KATE *and* BING *jump apart.* KATE *moves to center*) I'm so glad to see you, dear. (*Embraces her.*)

KATE

Thank you, m'am. (*Kisses* MRS. BROOKS) How have you been?

MRS. BROOKS

Just fine. Your mother tells me you're getting along splendidly with your position.

43

KATE

Yes, m'am.

MRS. BROOKS

(*Crosses to above divan, between* BING *and* KATE)
Sort of left you here all alone, didn't they, Bing?

BING

Yes, m'am ... sort of ... but ...

MRS. BROOKS

I guess that's all right with you, though.

BING

(*Self-consciously fidgeting around*)
Yes, m'am ... I don't mind bein' alone. ...

MRS. BROOKS

(*Smiling, she goes to door*)
Well, if you'll excuse me ... I'll be getting back to my turn-overs. Besides it's always customary to let the visiting team have a little infield practice. (*Goes into house.*)

BING

(*Crosses above divan to* KATE, *puts his hands on her waist*)
Well, Kate ... I'd like to sit around with you ... and just talk. But it's gettin' late ... and ...

KATE

Yes, I know, Bing. ... But ... there's something I've got to tell you about ...

BING

All right ... but ... better hurry.

44

KATE

I ... I quit my job. (*Crosses to divan.*)

BING

Quit your job? I thought you liked it in Roanoke.

KATE

(*Sits on divan*)

I've got to go away....

BING

Go away?

KATE

I wasn't going to tell you till it was all over....

BING

What do you mean?

KATE

Bing ... (*She sobs lightly.* BING *kneels beside her.*)

BING

C'mon now, Kate ... Don't cry, honey.... What's happened?

KATE

Oh, Bing ... I don't know how to tell you....

BING

What?

KATE

I'm ... I'm ... going to have a baby. (BING *is speechless, as if struck between the eyes. He looks at* KATE *for a moment. Then, as the full impact of the news hits him, he starts to mutter vaguely.)*

BING

Baby... (*Pause*) Great day in the morning.

KATE

(*Finds* BING's *hands*)

Oh, Bing...I'm so sorry...I didn't mean to tell you until you'd graduated...but I had to. I've got to go away. If they find out you're married, you'll be dismissed. (*One long blast from bugle off stage is heard.* BING *is too dazed to hear it.*)

BING

Baby...when did...when will...

KATE

In June....I'm going away tomorrow.

BING

(*Rises*)

I'm going with you....

KATE

(*Rises*)

No you're not. I'll be all right....You've got to graduate... especially now....

BING

But what'll you do? Where you gonna stay?

KATE

I found a place in Staunton.

46

BING

But you'll need money....

KATE

I'll manage....

BING

Here...I'll...(*Reaches into inside pocket of blouse, remembers he gave money to* BILLY. KATE *crosses to chaise-longue.*)

KATE
(*Restraining him*)

No, Bing...I won't take your money....You need it more than I....

BING

No one needs money more than you do....I'll send a check uptown...soon as I get back to barracks.

KATE

No, Bing...I wouldn't feel right....

BING
(*Crosses to* KATE)

You've got to take it....It'll get you out of town and keep you going for a while....If I can only graduate...

KATE

You've got to graduate and you will....

BING
(*In a haze*)

Yeah...(*Pause.*)

47

KATE

I hope it's a boy....

BING

(*Still in a fog*)

I don't know....

KATE

(*Trying to cheer him*)

If he'll only look like you...

BING

(*Vague*)

Oh, Kate...

KATE

When he grows up, he's going to be an athlete.

BING

I don't know.... Maybe he'd be better off being a grind.

KATE

He's going to win a Phi Beta Kappa key, but he's going to be an athlete, too. (*The sound of a bugle, blowing assembly, knocks* BING *out of his trance. Assembly is repeated, increasing in volume and tempo to curtain.*)

BING

Assembly... Migawd... Parade... (*Starts to go, stops at gate*) Gee... good-bye... Kate, I'll see you... When will I see you?

KATE

I...uh...don't know...I'll write you.... (MRS. BROOKS *enters quickly.*)

48

MRS. BROOKS

Bing ... You've got to run ... Assembly's gone. ....

BING

Yeah ... I know ... (*Rushes through gate.*)

KATE

But, Bing ...

MRS. BROOKS
(*Calling loudly*)

Bing ... your cap. ....

BING
(*Stopping*)

Yeah ... my cap ... (*Looks about madly*) Where is it?

KATE

Where did you put it?

MRS. BROOKS
(*Calling*)

Jenny ... Jenny ... (JENNY *enters*) Mr. Edwards' cap.

JENNY

Lord Almighty.

KATE

Never mind it, Bing ... go on. .... (BING *runs madly about, looking for his cap.*)

MRS. BROOKS

(*Spies cap on chair*) There ... (*Crossing to chair.*)

49

KATE

(*Pointing to cap*)

There!

JENNY

I got it. (*Runs to chair*) It's worse than a meeting of the Holy Rollers.

BING

Yeah.... (BING *rushes across stage.* MRS. BROOKS *grabs cap, hands it to* JENNY, *who meets* BING *center and gives him cap.* BING *rushes through gate and off.*)

KATE

Run, Bing...Run....

MRS. BROOKS

Yes, Bing, run....

JENNY

(*Stands center, gesticulating madly, looking after* BING) Run, white boy, run, run, run....

Curtain

ACT ONE

Scene II

That night, immediately after supper.

Scene: *A first classman's room in barracks. It is a bleak-looking room with buff-colored plaster walls. There is a wash basin with mirror and shelves for toilet articles on wall above. On right wall are a row of jade-green bookshelves filled with text-books. In back wall on a jog facing half right there is a jade-green door, the upper part of which contains glass partitions. It leads to the ground-floor stoop and courtyard of barracks. Along the right wall is a row of three steel lockers, containing towels, underclothing and personal articles. Left of lockers on wall, there are three hooks, hanging from which are three webbed field belts and three laundry bags. There are three mattresses, rolled, strapped and stacked along the left wall. On top of the mattresses is a pile of neatly folded blankets. Along the back wall, there are three wardrobe compartments painted jade green. On the floor beneath the wardrobes there is a shoe rack, also jade green, on top of which are several pairs of shoes and slippers. On top of the compartments are three cadet shakos, two of them equipped with ordinary pompoms, the third with a large feathered plume. On left wall there is a rifle rack painted jade green, with a U.S. army officer's sabre lying in the top groove, and two U.S. army rifles in the lower grooves. Two wooden cots, folded, and stacked on end against each other, lean against upstage section of left wall. In wall, right, there are casement windows in three sections, opening on stage. There is*

51

*an ordinary house broom with pine handle, leaning against the
left side of the wardrobe compartments. Small steam radiator,
left of wardrobe compartments. There is a small wooden jade-
green shining stool near the wash basin. Near the window, left,
there is a cot standing on the floor ready for use. A blanket
has been hastily thrown on top of its springs. In the center of
the room is a large square table. Hanging from the ceiling, a
few feet over the table, there is a drop light, covered with a
jade-green metal shade. Three cane wicker chairs, around the
table, complete the furniture in the room.*

BILLY *enters with his roommate* DAN CRAWFORD, *who is about
22 years old, average size, a stocky Northerner, and moderately
good-looking. In temper and mental alertness, he strikes the
mean between his two roommates,* BILLY *and* BING. *They are
arguing as they enter.*

BILLY

Well, how could I help it?

DAN

You shouldn't have left him.

BILLY

Shouldn't have left him.... What does he need—a chaperon?

DAN

Anything is liable to happen to him when he gets with that
girl of his. (*During this conversation,* BILLY *has been taking off
his blouse,* DAN *has put his cap on top of lockers.*)

BILLY

I told him to hurry.

52

DAN

Where is he now?

BILLY

How do I know? I'm no G-man.

DAN

Of all the stupid exhibitions ... galloping across the parade ground ... giving them this.... (*He illustrates by jumping up and down in place, wagging his head from side to side, while doing a succession of rapid-fire salutes*) In front of the whole staff of officers.

BILLY

(*Laughing, crosses to cot*)

Geez.... Thought I'd shed my feathers.... He sure made a shambles of that formation. (*He lies down on cot.* A. FURMAN TOWNSEND, JR., *enters. He is about 21 years old, a first-classman, a little backward in a worldly way, extremely naïve for a cadet, and the butt of many jokes from his classmates. He is a question-asker at heart.*)

TOWNSEND

(*Excited*)

Hey, fellas ...

DAN

What do you want, Townsend?

TOWNSEND

Did you know Bing missed parade?

BILLY

Townsend, if your brain was a whistle, you'd be silent as night. (*Throws himself down on cot.*)

53

TOWNSEND

Well...I didn't know.... You might have been excused...

DAN

For what? Nobody died. (DAN *removes his blouse, exposing his bare chest and two detachable cuffs hanging on wrists. He removes cuffs, hangs up blouse and puts on bathrobe.*)

TOWNSEND
(*Sits at table*)

Ah, don't be a Weisenheimer. Yeah, and I'll bet the Commandant would have had a few words to say to him if it wasn't he had to pitch tomorrow.

BILLY

You're always looking on the dark side of life, Townsend. (*Bugle heard blowing call to quarters.*)

DAN

Call to quarters. Better put up your hay, Billy. Lace drawers is on O. C. tonight. He'll see it through the window if he makes an inspection.

BILLY

No hurry. (TRIPOD ANDREWS *and* NEWSREEL SCOTT *enter.* ANDREWS *is a first-classman, likes to consider himself quite jaded and very mature for his 22 years.* SCOTT *is the enthusiastic manager of the baseball team, also a first-classman about 22 years old. He wears glasses.*)

SCOTT

How about Ty Cobb? He always slid head first.

54

DAN

What's the dope, manager?

SCOTT

Everything's all set...just talked to the coach....Bing pitches tomorrow and he'll stand those guys on their ears.

TOWNSEND

That's the way I figured it.

ANDREWS

What the hell do you know about it?

TOWNSEND

Plenty. I played a little ball...in my day.

ANDREWS

Where?

TOWNSEND
(*With his thumb*)

Back home.

BILLY

On the Boy Scout team in Beaver Falls, Pennsylvania.

TOWNSEND
(*Hurt*)

We all can't come from New York City....There's some pretty big men came out of Beaver Falls.

ANDREWS

Name one.

BILLY
(*Holds up one finger*)
Just one.

TOWNSEND
(*Crowded*)
Well ... it's a darn good town. (ANDREWS *crosses to window seat.*)

BILLY
That's not a town.... It's a mail box. (GRANT BOTTOME *slides into the room, removing his cap as he enters. He is a fourth-classman, about 17 years old, dressed in fatigue uniform, and remains in a Finn-out position, on his toes, his chin tucked in, his forearms parallel to the floor, palms facing the ceiling.*)

DAN
Sit down, Mistol.... What do you want? (BOTTOME *relaxes to normal standing position.*)

BOTTOME
Mr. Howard wants to borrow your Spanish book, sir. (DAN *crosses to bookshelves*) Says he can't find his own, sir. (*No answer.*)

ANDREWS
(*Looking out of window*)
Boy, did you ever see so many good-looking babies pouring in?

SCOTT
Yeah, the highways are full of 'em....
56

BILLY

And there's a lot more in the woods.

SCOTT

That's one thing you have to hand this place.... When the man-handlers start flocking in, they really *flock*.

DAN

(*Running through pages of a book and removing odd pieces of paper*)

Tell him to get it back before tattoo.

BOTTOME

I'll tell him, sir. (*Exits.*)

SCOTT

Hey, Tripod ... Is that blonde pooper-dooper of yours from Richmond down for the week-end?

BILLY

Yeah, how about that slow-ball?

ANDREWS

C'est fini la guerre! She started to turn out the standard bundle.

BILLY

The little white house with the little green blinds at the end of honeymoon lane.

ANDREWS

And how!

TOWNSEND

Women can certainly have funny ideas.

DAN

(*Taking a very dirty shirt from pile of laundry, calls to* BILLY)
You must have been wearing my sweat shirt. (*Tosses it right of locker*) Trying to contaminate my laundry? (BILLY *disregards him.*)

TOWNSEND

You know there's one thing I can't understand about women. I mean like now, for instance. After a fellow's been expecting something—a letter from a person for two weeks—over two weeks—and you wrote this person and wanted to know what the matter is—but you didn't get an answer from this person—does that mean anything?

ANDREWS

Don't worry about it, Towse. Time will tell. (*Drum heard off stage.*)

ANDREWS
(*Crosses in front of table*)
Come on, Newsreel, call to quarters.

TOWNSEND

You know what we are—just slaves to a system. (ANDREWS, SCOTT *and* TOWNSEND *exit.* DAN *gets books, sits at table, starts to study.*)

BILLY
(*From recumbent position on cot*)
Say, Dan . . .

58

DAN
(*Without looking up*)

Yeah? What do you want?

BILLY

Oh, I just wanted to tell you something.

DAN
(*Suspiciously*)

What?

BILLY
(*Sitting up*)

Joyce is in town.

DAN

I hope she'll be very happy. (*Goes back to his studying. There is a knock on the door.*)

VOICE OF OFFICER OF THE DAY
(*Off stage*)

Report!

BILLY *and* DAN
(*Jump to their feet*)

All right, sir.

BILLY

Hey, Dan, you know what?

DAN

No, what?

BILLY

I think it was her grandmother that threw the hammers into the machinery. (DAN *continues to study*) I saw her this afternoon. Joyce, I mean. Well, I saw the grandmother too, but I mean ...

DAN

Shut up awhile, will you? I want to study.

BILLY

No, but this is important. I'm going to do my best to make her week-end a success, and you might help me out if you want to. She's invited me over to see her at her grandmother's.

DAN

When?

BILLY

Tonight after taps.... (DAN *grunts, turns around in chair, facing front*) And, listen, Dan, she brought along her roommate.

DAN

(*Emphatically*)

Stop right there!

BILLY

Now, wait a minute, this girl is a great little number.

DAN

Not interested. I've been on blind dates with you before.

BILLY

That's a fine thing to say.

60

DAN

And what's more, I got a ball game to catch tomorrow.

BILLY

And I've been on blind dates with you too. (*Arguing*) And the last time you sucked me in for that Peggy what-the-hell-ever-her-name-is from the State Teachers' College. She didn't have enough sex appeal to flag a hand car.

DAN
(*Faces* BILLY)

That was different ...

BILLY

I didn't have a ball game to catch the next day, but I had a Calculus exam to get ready for. And doing daily derivatives would have been a picnic compared to the deadly hours with that All-American shot-putter. (HARLEY HARRINGTON *enters*.)

DAN

Hello, Harley.

HARRINGTON

Hello, Dan.

BILLY
(*Turning around*)

Oh, hello, Harley. How's the war lord?

HARRINGTON

I'm all right ... Say, Billy ... I asked a girl down for the week-end ... But you know all about that, don't you?

61

BILLY

Yeah ... Someone was telling me ... Joyce Winfree.

HARRINGTON

I stopped around to take her to parade this afternoon, and she wasn't there. It seems as if ...

BILLY

(Rises and crosses to cot)

I'll tell you how that happened, Harley. I just happened to drop by there with Bing.... She was waiting for you, and ...

HARRINGTON

That's all right ... Don't bother ... Only ... The reason I asked her down for the week-end ... was because I wanted to spend some time with her ...

BILLY

(Sits on cot)

I don't blame you, she's ...

HARRINGTON

So, if it's all the same with you, let me plan her itinerary, will you?

BILLY

Sure, Harley. Go right ahead.... No hard feelings?

HARRINGTON

None at all, but I just thought I'd make myself clear.

BILLY

Sure ... Set your mind at ease ... You've got the play of the field ... I wouldn't lay a glove on her. (BING *enters—in a fog.*)

HARRINGTON

Oh, hello, Bing.

BING

Hello, Harley. (HARRINGTON *exits.*)

DAN

Where you been?

BING

I was walking around—thinking.

BILLY
(*Good-naturedly*)
Turning philosopher on us, huh? (TOWNSEND *rushes in.*)

TOWNSEND
(*Excited*)
Hey, fellas ... fellas ...

DAN
(*Slams hand on table*)
Are you in again!

TOWNSEND

Listen, fellas ...

BILLY

What's the matter now?

TOWNSEND
(*Excited*)
There's a guy uptown at the Stonewall Jackson Hotel taking
all bets on the game ... Even money ...

BILLY

Even money, eh?

DAN

And I gave four to three yesterday.

TOWNSEND

And now they're offering even money. What do you suppose that means? Does that mean anything? Everybody in barracks is laying money down.... My roommate just bet thirty bucks ... and I bet all *I* had ...

BILLY

How much?

TOWNSEND

Two and a half.... Slim is burning the tires up on that old taxi takin' those bets uptown.

BILLY

Gee, I wish I had some dough....

TOWNSEND

Dan, do you think we'll win?

DAN

Sure I do. We've got to win....

BILLY

I wouldn't miss that game tomorrow for all the dogs in Georgia.

TOWNSEND

Boy, I'm glad Bing's gonna pitch.... Well ... I'll see you later. Talk about excitement, gee. (*Exits.* BING *crosses to door.*)

DAN

Where you goin' now?

BING

(*As he exits*)

I'm goin' out and think some more.

BILLY

That boy is certainly in a fog. Say, Danny boy, you haven't any spare cash, have you? (DAN *gives him a slow look, then resumes his studying*) No, this is serious.

DAN

(*Looks up—serious*)

Listen, Brother Rat, I've been buying your way out of crap games and financing your block-running expeditions for four years ... and if I had any money now I wouldn't give it to you ... so get off my ear.

BILLY

I wish my old man'd hurry up and send that check. Should have been here yesterday. It's not my fault people stop reading books.

DAN

What the devil do you *do* with it all, anyway?

BILLY

I give it to the poor.

DAN

If I was your father, I'd kick your tail all the way to Buena Vista and back. You don't know how much you have to sweat

65

to earn a dollar bill.... That's virgin territory to you.... *I* can't write home for money every time the spirit moves me.... My old man's being strangled to death by a white collar in Bridge-port, Connecticut. Cripes, the way you tear through a saw-buck you'd think your old man owned a bank.

BILLY

Listen, Dan, we're gonna win that ball game tomorrow, aren't we?

DAN

Sure we are, but ...

BILLY

That's all I wanted to know. (*Goes to window, whistles, motions to someone to come over.*)

DAN

What do you want that guy for?

BILLY

I got fifty bucks here that belongs to Bing. I was gonna de-posit it for him but I forgot and now I got a great idea. I'll double his money first. (*Leans over table, making his point to* DAN) If *you* had any dough, you'd bet it on tomorrow's game, wouldn't you? Well, I know you would, 'cause you did. And you're an insider. You're in the know. So if you ...

DAN

I bet my own money but not Bing's.

BILLY

Do you realize how much Bing needs dough?

66

DAN

'Course I do.

BILLY

Well, I'm not letting this money lie around in a third-rate bank drawing two percent.

SLIM

(*Enters through window.* SLIM *is a cadaverous-looking fellow about 35 years old, dressed in gray cadet riding breeches, leggings, gray flannel shirt, dark blue windbreaker, dark gray taxi driver's cap. Talks with Southern drawl*) Y'all want me?

BILLY

Come in, Slim. (*Gets money from blouse in wardrobe compartment.*)

SLIM

Coming. Y'all having financial troubles again, Brother Rat Randolph? (BILLY *crosses to* SLIM.)

BILLY

Just a little deal, Slim. Listen.... There's a guy uptown at the Stonewall Jackson covering all bets for the game tomorrow.

SLIM

Gotcha...

BILLY

Dig him up, get the best odds you can... and bet this on VMI... right on the button.... (*Gives* SLIM *the money.*)

SLIM

Gotcha.... (*Starts toward window.*)

BILLY

And don't get caught going out that window.

SLIM

(*Stops*)

I been sitting in my taxi out in front o' that there arch, and climbin' in and outta these windows for the last fo'teen years, and nobody caught me yet. (*Looks out window, then climbs out.* BILLY *watches him go, then looks at* DAN. DAN *looks disgustedly at* BILLY.)

BILLY

Listen, Dan, don't be worried about it. It was really the conservative thing to do. Bing has got everything to gain and nothing to lose. (TOWNSEND *enters joyously.*)

TOWNSEND

Boy, oh boy, I just got a special. (*Holds up letter.*)

DAN

Humpin' bumpin' jumpin'—Jearuselum! Please stay home, will you, Towse; they gave you a room.

TOWNSEND

Look at what I got. You know what I was telling you that a certain person hadn't written me for two weeks. It was all just a mistake.... And now I got a special.

DAN

Don't you know they've blown call to quarters?

TOWNSEND

(*Jumping on window seat*)

The heck with that. Gwendolyn is coming down for graduation. Only two more months and she'll be here. (*Dances toward*

68

table) Oh, boy...No kidding, she's the sweetest gal I've ever seen.

DAN

Put a nickel in the slot and the same thing happens every time.

TOWNSEND

Don't worry. When the right one comes along you'll fall too.

DAN

Why should I? There's other things in life besides women. My God! Don't you ever stop to reason it out?

TOWNSEND
(*Sincerely*)

Yes, I did. When she didn't write me I tried to reason it out ...but I don't know...when you get that gnawing feeling down here, and you haven't any appetite...and you try to eat ...but you can't eat...and when you do...(*A sharp rap is heard on the door. Lieutenant "Lace Drawers" ROGERS enters. He is about 30 years old, tall and awkward. His carriage is non-military. He would be more at home as a professor in a civilian college rather than an officer and instructor in a military college. He is dressed in a lieutenant's U. S. Army uniform. He carries a folded piece of paper in one hand and a pencil in the other. All jump to attention as he enters. They stand naturally, not like tin soldiers. He speaks authoritatively, but not menacingly.*)

ROGERS

Visiting, Townsend?

TOWNSEND

Yes, sir...but...

ROGERS

But what?

TOWNSEND

Uh ... nothing, sir ... just visiting ...

ROGERS

During call to quarters ... Drive on to your room.

TOWNSEND

Yes, sir. (*Exits.*)

ROGERS
(*Writes. Sees cot down*)
Who's responsible for that cot being down?

BILLY

I am, sir.

ROGERS

You know better than to have a cot down before ten o'clock. Put it up. (BILLY *crosses to cot, folds it and starts to stand it up against the others.*)

ROGERS
(*Writing*)
Your initials are W. J., aren't they?

BILLY

That's right.

ROGERS

What was that?

70

BILLY

Yes, sir ... That's right, sir ... W. J., sir.

ROGERS

Straighten this room up some.

DAN

Yes, sir. (*They start straightening up the table, as* ROGERS *exits, and stop as soon as he has left the room.*)

BILLY

I'll bet his mother's proud of him. Crawford, am I a man or a mouse?

DAN

(*Quickly*)

Mouse.

BILLY

Lieutenant Lace Drawers Rogers. You know it's guys like that who are responsible for peace movements being started.

DAN

It would have been just as easy to put your hay up before.

BILLY

Well, I forgot.

DAN

Well, he reminded you.

BILLY

He could have been more subtle about it.

71

DAN

What do you want from the guy? He has to earn a living, too.

BILLY

Why doesn't he get a job as house mother at the Mary Baldwin School for Girls?

DAN

All right, shut up.

BILLY

I will in just a second. Listen, Dan, about tonight... (DAN *shuts book in disgust*) I wouldn't have the nerve to ask you if this girl didn't qualify. I saw her this afternoon.... I tell you she's all right.

DAN

What do you mean, all right.

BILLY

Well, she's no Miss America... but she's got plenty on the ball and a *swell personality*.

DAN

Sorry... Can't swing it. (*Pause.*)

BILLY

All right, Brother Rat, if you want to let me down.

DAN

I don't want to let you down, Billy, but...

BILLY

(*So sincere*)

Only I remember four years ago when you were lying right in that cot, so sick you couldn't bat a fly off the wall...and I skipped parade to sneak uptown to get you some orange juice. You made some swell promises then...anything I wanted, write my own ticket.

DAN

You go a long way back to cite cases.

BILLY

(*Leaning over table to make his point*)

And I could tell you something recent.

DAN

No, don't bother, just shut up....I'll go.

BILLY

(*Patting* DAN *on his back*)

That's great, Danny boy.

DAN

You get the rats to sleep in our hay!

BILLY

(*Confident*)

Sure, I'll fix it.

DAN

And we're coming home early.

BILLY

Oh, absolutely. (TOWNSEND *rushes in, followed by two* CADETS.)

73

TOWNSEND

Hey, what do you know? The Commandant sent for Bing.

BILLY

What?

TOWNSEND

He's going to make him walk penalty tours because he missed parade this afternoon.

DAN

(*Gets up*)

What'd you say?

TOWNSEND

Yeah, ain't that terrible? Bing can't pitch tomorrow.

BILLY

He's gotta pitch.... He's got money on the game.

TOWNSEND

He can't.... He's got to walk penalty tours. I think it's terrible.... It's an outrage. I feel like committing suicide.

DAN

My God! You mean old Ramm-rod is goin' to keep him from pitching?

CADETS

Yeah!

BILLY

Somebody's gotta *do* somethin'.... I'll go up there and see Ramm-rod myself. (*Starts toward wardrobe compartment.*)

74

DAN

You keep out of it.

TOWNSEND

Newsreel is up there now. He's trying to persuade him. (BING *enters, beaten*) Gee, Bing, that's terrible.

BILLY

What'd he say to you?

BING

I gotta walk penalty tours.

BILLY

But the game... You gotta pitch.... You don't know how important it is.

DAN

Can't you walk them later on? (BING *shakes his head*.)

BING

Tomorrow...

BILLY

Didn't you argue with him?

BING

The Commandant?

BILLY

But, my God, we can't take this lying down. This is the twentieth century ... not the Spanish Inquisition. (SCOTT *rushes in*.)

75

SCOTT

Hey! Here comes Ramm-rod.

BILLY

What?

SCOTT

I've been over talking to him. He's coming here to see Bing.

BILLY

(*Excited*)

Get out of here, you guys.

TOWNSEND

Oh, baby, I should say. (TOWNSEND *and the two* CADETS *exit hurriedly.*)

BING

What's he gonna do?

SCOTT

I don't know but I've been working on him. He's on the way over. For God's sake, be careful. (*Rushes out.*)

BING

What'll I say?

BILLY

Don't say anything...look humble.... (*To* DAN) And you study and I'll shine brass. (*Crosses to above table, looking for shining board. A sharp rap on the door is heard. There is a hush as* COLONEL RAMM *enters. The boys snap to attention.* COLONEL RAMM *is about fifty years old, well built, important-*

76

looking, has a fine military carriage and speaks with the authority of a Colonel in the U. S. Army. He is dressed in an officers' uniform with boots and Sam Browne belt.)

RAMM

Mr. Edwards.

BING

Yes, sir.

RAMM

Your conduct this afternoon was very unorthodox.

BING

Yes, sir. (BILLY *and* DAN *look straight ahead.*)

RAMM

You're a grown man, Mr. Edwards, and this is not a prep school or a country club.

BING

Yes, sir.

RAMM

I have assigned you your penalty and it cannot be retracted. (*Slight pause*) But, although it is against my principles to allow extra-curricular activities to interfere with daily routine...in view of your importance on the baseball team...and tomorrow's game...I was a cadet once myself...I have consented to allow you to participate...if you walk your penalty tours tonight....Is this clear? (BILLY *and* DAN *smile.*)

BING

Yes, sir.

RAMM

Very well. (*Takes a step toward door, halts and resumes*)
I hope, Mr. Edwards, hereafter your conduct will be more be-
coming to your position in the corps and the respect which it
behooves you to retain.

BING

Yes, sir.

RAMM

Carry on. (*Exits.*)

BILLY

(*Shaking* DAN's *hand—happy*)
A heart of gold.

DAN

That guy's a gentleman. You can pitch. Now, listen, let's not
waste any time. You get right out there and start pounding
those bricks so you'll be done in time to get some sleep tonight.

BING

I can't sleep. (*Helplessly*) She didn't want to worry me.

DAN

Listen, Bing, you gotta pitch tomorrow. You mustn't worry
about *anything*.

BING

I gotta worry.

BILLY

You mean it's mandatory?

78

BING

I can't pitch. I'm married.

BILLY
(*Hit by a bomb*)

You're *what*?

DAN
(*Amazed*)

Married? You're not *kiddin'*?

BING

No ... honest.

BILLY

Kate?

BING

Yeah.

DAN

When?

BING

Last Fall.

BILLY
(*Pounding it home*)

If they ever find this out the Commandant'll ship you in
fifteen minutes.

DAN

Does anyone know?

79

BING
(Nods head slowly)

Kate knows.

BILLY

Well, she ought to.

DAN

Anyone else?

BING

No.

DAN

If you ever kept your mouth shut, you'd better do it now.

BING

I can't understand it....

BILLY

What?

BING

Kate's gonna have a baby.

DAN
(Takes a step back)
Going...to...have...a...baby. (BILLY *slumps into chair.*)

BILLY
(Sinks into chair)
A drug store on every corner in America and you go and ring up a baby.

Curtain

ACT TWO

ACT TWO

Scene I

About an hour later that night.

Scene: *Porch, same as Act One, Scene I.* BILLY *and* DAN *are dressed in white paletots, consisting of white duck trousers, white shirt, black four-in-hand tie, white duck English cut blouse with brass buttons, and brass military insignia on lapels of blouse.*

DAN *and* CLAIRE *are sitting on divan.* BILLY *and* JOYCE *are sitting on the forward section of chaise-longue facing* DAN *and* CLAIRE.

BILLY
(In full swing)

... and the devil pats me on the shoulder and says, "My good friend Randolph, take charge of the detail." So I walks up to the first guy and says you look mighty familiar to me. What's your name and he says "Lace Drawers," and I says "Ha-a-a, Lace Drawers, I've been waiting thirty-five years for you. I always knew I was going to hell, but I was never sure I'd be a third-classman when you got here. (BILLY *laughs loudly at his joke, the girls giggle and* DAN *lets out a forced horse laugh, showing his general disgust.*)

JOYCE
And then you woke up?

83

BILLY

Yes, and was darned near late for breakfast formation.

CLAIRE

Are you sure Lieutenant Rogers won't be waiting for you when you get back to barracks tonight?

DAN
(*Looking for an out*)
If you're worried, we can leave now.

CLAIRE
(*Looks at* DAN)
I thought a VMI man could cope with any situation.

BILLY

Never even heard of VMI.... A moon, the stars, and a gorgeous slowball.

DAN

Just a poet at heart.

JOYCE
(*Puzzled*)
Slowball?

DAN

In Billy's vernacular, a slowball's a blonde. (CLAIRE *giggles. Then to* CLAIRE) That makes you a fastball. (BILLY *rises, assumes stance of batter at plate, facing audience.*)

BILLY

Here I am ... with my bat in my hand ... looking the field over.... Here she comes ... not fast, no hop ... just floatin' right

in there easy like.... I see her comin'.... I get a toehold and ...
(BILLY *swings imaginary bat in air.*)

DAN
(*Solemnly*)

Strike one!

BILLY
(*A dirty look to* DAN, *then leans on imaginary bat*)
Strike one.... (*To* JOYCE) Just a sucker for a slowball. (*Both girls are amused,* DAN *bored.* BILLY *dusts off plate with imaginary cap, puts it back on head, knocks dirt off spikes with bat, hitches up his pants, in true baseball player's fashion, and resumes stance at plate*) Now, the pitcher changes his pace.... (*He looks out into the audience as if waiting for the pitch*) She's coming right at me.... (*BILLY does not see* MRS. BROOKS *as she enters*) A sizzling, roaring fastball. (*Sees* MRS. BROOKS *and backs up.* JOYCE, DAN *and* CLAIRE *rise as* MRS. BROOKS *enters.*)

CLAIRE
Hello, Mrs. Brooks. (BILLY *and* JOYCE, *slightly embarrassed, turn.*)

MRS. BROOKS
Good evening.

JOYCE
Hello, Grandma.

BILLY
Good evening, Mrs. Brooks.

JOYCE
Do you know Dan Crawford?

MRS. BROOKS

With a four hundred batting average? I should say I do.

DAN

(*Shakes hands with her*)

How do you do, Mrs. Brooks?

MRS. BROOKS

I'm fine, thank you.

BILLY

Certainly is nice to see you, Mrs. Brooks. (BILLY *brings chair*)
Won't you sit down?

MRS. BROOKS

(*Not too enthusiastically*)

Thank you. (DAN *and* CLAIRE *sit on divan.* JOYCE *sits on chaise-
longue facing* MRS. BROOKS. *To* BILLY) Weren't you explaining
something?

BILLY

No, ma'am....

MRS. BROOKS

When I arrived.

BILLY

I mean...uh...I'd finished.

MRS. BROOKS

(*Proud of her knowledge of baseball terms*)

Well, I was watching you and I'll tell you one thing. You'll
never hit a fast ball if you keep putting your foot in the bucket.

(DAN *and* BILLY *force a laugh*) I stopped off at Mrs. Rice's after the movies.

JOYCE

Was Kate home?

MRS. BROOKS
(*To* JOYCE)
Yes, and I can't get over the way she's picked up. (DAN *looks at* BILLY. BILLY *lets out an audible gasp, then covers it by coughing. Sits down beside* JOYCE.)

CLAIRE

Why, Billy ...

JOYCE

Would you like some water?

BILLY
(*Coming out of the cough*)
No ... thank you ... I just ... uh ... hit a rock.

MRS. BROOKS

Kate sure was looking blue this afternoon when Bing dashed off to parade.

JOYCE

I'll bet she was.

MRS. BROOKS

As if she was standing on third base with the weak end of the batting list coming up. (*Boys laugh politely.*)

87

JOYCE

I thought she might come over tonight.

MRS. BROOKS

She had a visitor.

JOYCE

Oh, did she?

DAN
(*Scared*)

Not Bing?

MRS. BROOKS

No. One of the younger officers.... I've never met him before
...Lieutenant Rogers.

BILLY
(*Spontaneously*)

Lace-Drawers.

MRS. BROOKS

What was that?

BILLY

Uh...Theodore.

MRS. BROOKS

That's a nice name. Lieutenant Theodore Rogers.

JOYCE

Hm, the Lieutenant's giving your roommate a little compe-
tition.

88

BILLY
(*Quietly but confident*)
I don't know ... Bing's got quite a lead on him.

MRS. BROOKS
Well, Claire, what do you think of the VMI cadets?

CLAIRE
Oh, I think they're perfect gentlemen.

BILLY
(*Half rising, with a slight bow*)
It's little things like that we live for.

MRS. BROOKS
You're in for a big thrill tomorrow, Claire. They're having Garrison Review.

CLAIRE
Yes, Joyce told me.

MRS. BROOKS
I never tire of watching that fine-looking corps of cadets marching onto the parade ground in such perfect rhythm, and standing so straight and upright in that long gray line.

JOYCE
I like it best after inspection. The band starts playing and the battalion moves as a unit, then breaks into each separate company and passes in review. (*Slight pause.*)

DAN
You sure know your VMI.

MRS. BROOKS

She ought to. Joyce was the prize baby of her father's class. (JOYCE *faces front like an embarrassed child*) The first one, you know, Claire. That's one of the nicest traditions of VMI. My son was the first alumnus in his class to become a father.

BILLY
(*To* JOYCE)

I always knew you were distinguished. (JOYCE *turns away from* BILLY *embarrassed.*)

MRS. BROOKS
(*Rises. All rise with her*)

Well, it's getting pretty late. (*Slyly*) I presume it's all right for you boys to be out of barracks at this hour?

BILLY
(*Reassuringly*)

Oh, yes, m'am.

MRS. BROOKS
(*To girls*)

Remember, girls, you have a full day ahead tomorrow, but of course ... VMI boys always know when to leave. (*She goes into the house.*)

BILLY
(*To group*)

Now, *that's* what you might call putting the umlaut on top of the O. (*All sit.* BILLY *last. There is a short pause.*)

CLAIRE
(*Innocently*)

Certainly is a beautiful night.

90

BILLY

One of the most romantic I've ever seen. (*Hinting*) What do you think, Dan?

DAN

(*Doesn't get it*)

Huh? Yeah ... Nice night. (*Pause.*)

JOYCE

Certainly is. ... (*Pause.*)

BILLY

Joyce, you know that rose arbor of your grandmother's in back of the house?

JOYCE

Yes?

BILLY

(*With innuendo*)

Have you seen it, Dan?

DAN

No.

BILLY

You seen it, Claire?

CLAIRE

No, I don't think I noticed.

BILLY

Mighty pretty. (*Pause.* BILLY, *whistling "Alone," rises. Whistles a few bars, looks at* DAN *then crosses to table.* BILLY *turns, spies book on top of table, near window. He picks it up, crosses to* DAN *and hands him the book.* DAN *looks at the book, looks at* BILLY, *then back at book.* CLAIRE *looks at book and laughs.*)

JOYCE
(*Baffled*)

What is it?

CLAIRE
(*Blushing and giggling*)
It Can't Happen Here, by Sinclair Lewis. (CLAIRE *gives book to* BILLY *who returns it to table.* JOYCE *smiles.*)

DAN
(*He rises*)
C'mon, Claire.... We'll take a walk. (*Takes her arm.*)

CLAIRE
(*Rising*)
All right. (*They start toward walk*) Where are we going?

DAN
(*As they exit*)
Let's take a look at that rose arbor. (BILLY *crosses to* JOYCE, *reaches over, gallantly takes her hand and helps her to rise. She acquiesces dubiously.*)

JOYCE
Are we going for a walk?

BILLY
(*Nodding head*)
Right to the divan. (*Hand in hand, they cross to divan.*)

92

JOYCE
(*Stops*)
Why the divan?

BILLY
When I was little bit of a boy, Joyce, my father always told me "Never stand up when you can sit down, and never sit down, when you can lie down." (*Points to divan*) And I've been sitting on that thing so long, I feel like a bareback rider.

JOYCE
I thought it was rather comfortable.

BILLY
Only a woman could be comfortable on a thing called a chaise-longue. Fellow like me, though, likes something rugged. (*Pats divan as they sit*) Like this divan, where I can stretch ... (*Sits*) relax, and breathe.... (*He takes a deep breath, reaches over, puts his arm about* JOYCE *and pulls her into a half reclining position. Half-heartedly she allows it. They remain for a moment in silence*) Yes, sir ... Joyce ... Relax ... (*Arm around her waist*) and breathe.... (*He becomes more amorous.*)

JOYCE
(*Removes his arm and pushes him away*)
Let's not take your father's advice too literally.

BILLY
(*Crosses to chair*)
Well, I was a blue-ribbon baby.

JOYCE
You know, Billy, in a way I'm sorry you came tonight. I mean if you get caught you'll have to ...

BILLY

You don't think I'd take the chance of running the block for anybody else?

JOYCE

I hate to see you take that risk, Billy, with only two months to go before graduation.

BILLY

(*Waxing eloquent*)

Lovely lady, for this moment, I'd swim the English Channel with my feet tied....

JOYCE

(*Feigns surprise*)

What, no millstone? (*Pause.* JOYCE *smiles, as* BILLY *continues.*)

BILLY

You hear that noise?

JOYCE

What noise?

BILLY

(*Puts hand on heart*)

That's the little wire buzzing inside of me. (*Looks at her enraptured*) "Never before have I beheld such bliss as the divine completeness of a kiss." (*Attempts to kiss* JOYCE *on lips. She turns her head. He tenderly kisses her forehead.*)

JOYCE

Pretty.

94

BILLY

You like it?

JOYCE

The poetry. Who wrote it?

BILLY

(*Never non-plussed*)

Dowson, a decadent poet. But I've got to have somebody to help me. (BILLY *tilts his head back ecstatically, breathes a deep sigh and takes his arm from* JOYCE. *Puts his cheek against hers, then slides to the floor, groaning with ecstasy. He puts his head in her lap*) Ah! My mother told me there'd be nights like this, but I never believed her. (JOYCE *smiles.* BILLY *leans back and gazes up to the ceiling. Smiles.* JOYCE *runs her fingers through his hair*) If the Commandant could only see me now.

JOYCE

(*Abruptly*)

How do you like the new Commandant?

BILLY

You're distracting me. After all, I'm only a simple soldier. Did you ever see a war?

JOYCE

A war?

BILLY

(*Rises*)

Yeah. When an army starts out with a certain objective, they generally approach it as a unit from the front, till they ... (*Gets*

95

closer) get within striking distance. (*Leans over and places hands on her legs. She removes his hands indignantly*) Then a personal reconnaissance is made. (*Kneels beside her on divan and tries to put his hand on her waist. She slaps his hand and he jumps back*) If they reach an impasse, they momentarily withdraw.... (*Crosses around divan and kisses the back of her neck*) Then they approach from the opposite flank. And launch a surprise attack. (*Leaps and lands half on* JOYCE *in a long embrace. She struggles, then embraces him as they kiss lingeringly.* DAN *and* CLAIRE *enter. They stand there for a moment, watching curiously.* CLAIRE *acts embarrassed.*)

DAN

Well! (BILLY *and* JOYCE *jump apart.* BILLY *sits beside her, pulling down his blouse and straightening his tie*) What a beautiful friendship!

CLAIRE
(*Sits in chair*)

Well, we're back.

BILLY
(*Annoyed*)

Back to back, like a pair of deuces.

JOYCE
(*Rises*)

Supposing I run in and get us something to eat?

BILLY
(*Catches* JOYCE's *hand*)

Don't leave me. I'm not hungry.

96

DAN

You look hungry. (*Ragging* BILLY) When you get that gnawing feeling down here ... you want to eat ... but you can't eat ... and when you do ...

JOYCE

(*Starts toward door*)
If you'll excuse me, I think I'll get a glass of water.

BILLY

(*Rises. Goes to* JOYCE)
Can't I get it for you?

JOYCE

No, thank you. (*Crosses to door and turns*) If you want to, you may come along and get it with me. (*Goes into house.* BILLY *goes to door and stops.*)

BILLY

(*Eloquently*)
I leave all this behind me. (*Goes into house.* CLAIRE *crosses to divan and sits.*)

DAN

(*Sits on chaise-longue*)
You see, I room with a fellow named Bing Edwards.... He's not very smart, but he's the greatest go-through guy I've ever known. I've been rooming with him since prep school, and he's been pitchin' to me for seven years.

CLAIRE

That's a long time.

DAN

It's a lot of pitchin'. There are two things he's been working for, since he hit this man's school: He wants to graduate—and that's a tough one for him—and he wants to win the award that's given to the best athlete in the class. It probably sounds silly to you to get sentimental over your roommate winning an athletic award.

CLAIRE

What is it, a cup?

DAN

Plus two hundred bucks. And if he's going to win this award he's got to be real sharp tomorrow. (*Pause*) That's probably the longest speech I ever made to a woman in my life.

CLAIRE

I've got an ambition, too.

DAN

What is it?

CLAIRE

I've always been interested in science. You spend your afternoons on a baseball field, I spend mine in a chemistry laboratory.

DAN

Chemistry? That's funny.

CLAIRE

Why?

98

DAN

Bing's majoring in chemistry—my roommate, you know.

CLAIRE

Is he?

DAN

You must like it a lot?

CLAIRE

Oh, I do, very much.

DAN

You're probably good at it.

CLAIRE

I'm afraid I am.... I want to be a bacteriologist.

DAN

You do?

CLAIRE

I hope to get a fellowship from the Rockefeller Foundation.

DAN

Oh, yeah. Where they have the guinea pigs?

CLAIRE

Yes, I like them. And although I'm no Venus de Milo, I like men too.

DAN

Well, that makes you normal.... (BILLY *peeps in*.)

BILLY

(*Happy*)

Well, well, look at those two dovetail—hand-in-glove...
(*Carries in tray of sandwiches and lemonade*) Great little kid,
isn't she, Danny boy? (BILLY *takes chair and carries it to divan.*)

DAN

(*Rises*)

Yeah. (*Starts to give pre-arranged signal*) Billy, the time has
come...

BILLY

(*Not getting it*)

We have plenty of time.

DAN

(*A little louder*)

The time has *come*...

BILLY

(*Still not getting it*)

You don't want to rush off in the heat of the day?

DAN

(*Slightly impatient*)

The walrus...*the walrus*...

BILLY

(*Getting it*)

Oh, the *walrus*...sure. (*He crosses to* JOYCE, *quickly says a
few words close to her ear.*)

JOYCE

Yes, of course, first door on the left.

BILLY

C'mon, Danny. (*He and* DAN *exit.* BILLY *starts to sing "Just a Kiss in the Dark."*)

JOYCE

(*Goes to door—calls inside*)

All right, Billy, we've been all over that. (*Crosses to divan*) Well, what do you think, Claire?

BILLY

(*Reappears in doorway*)

Wait till we get to the first landing 'fore you start talking about us. (*Disappears from door.*)

JOYCE

What do you think?

CLAIRE

Which one—yours or mine?

JOYCE

Billy.

CLAIRE

Well ... He's crazy as a quilt, but ...

JOYCE

Yes, but he's cute. What do you think of Dan?

CLAIRE

Well, he's a baseball catcher ... not exactly what I expected, but I think I like him. (*They hear footsteps.* JOYCE *sees who is approaching, and gasps.* COLONEL RAMM *enters.* JOYCE *tries to make the door.* CLAIRE *jumps up*) Why, *Dad!*

RAMM

(*Goes to* JOYCE)

Hello, Claire. Hello, Joyce.

JOYCE

(*Panicky*)

Uh...good evenin', Colonel Ramm.

RAMM

You'll have to excuse me for coming in at this hour, but I have to round up my daughter.

CLAIRE

How did you...?

RAMM

I saw the lights on the porch, and thought you and Joyce would be up talking. (*To* CLAIRE) Are you ready to go in the morning?

CLAIRE

(*Crosses to* RAMM, *takes his hand to start him off*)

Yes, Dad. I'm all ready. (*Trying to rush him off*) Well, good night, Joyce.

RAMM

(*With quiet dignity*)

Now, just a minute....I haven't seen Joyce since the midwinter dances, and I know she won't mind.... (*Sits on divan.*)

JOYCE

Not at all....Let me get you a drink or something.... (*Starts toward door.*)

102

RAMM

(*Checking her*)

Now, you come right back here, child. You don't need to en-tertain me. (JOYCE *hesitatingly returns to divan*) Joyce, how would you like to drive to Roanoke with Claire and me tomorrow morning?

JOYCE

(*Quickly*)

Thank you, Colonel ... I'd love it. (*She rises, but* RAMM *has her hand and pulls her down beside him on divan.*)

RAMM

(*Slowly*)

I have to pick up the Third Corps Area Inspector. We'll be back by Garrison Review tomorrow afternoon, so you won't miss anything.

JOYCE

(*Rises. Speaks rapidly.* CLAIRE *rises*)

Thank you, Colonel ... very much ... uh ... Claire, call me in the morning when you're ready to leave. (*Agitated*) If you'll excuse me for a moment ... (*Starts toward door.*)

RAMM

Don't rush off. We're leaving anyhow. (JOYCE *stops*) We have to get to bed if ...

CLAIRE

(*Anxious to get him off. Pulls him from divan*)

Yes, Dad ... We'd better go. ... (COLONEL RAMM *looks questioningly at his daughter, then smiles as he turns to* JOYCE.)

RAMM

Well...uh...good night, Joyce. We'll pick you up in the morning.

JOYCE

Thank you, Colonel....I'll be... (*Shakes* RAMM's *hand.* BILLY *starts singing off stage.*)

CLAIRE

(*Quickly shakes hands with* JOYCE. *They start toward the right side of porch*)

'Night, Joyce....Come along, Dad....We... (JOYCE *starts toward door.* BILLY, *singing "With My Eyes Wide Open," enters.* COLONEL RAMM *hears the singing, stops and looks toward door as* BILLY *enters.*)

BILLY

(*He spies Commandant and stops dead in his tracks*)
God! (BILLY *stands at rigid attention. The girls freeze.*)

RAMM

(*Changes from the good-natured parent to the rigid disciplinarian*)
Well, this is very unorthodox, Mr. Randolph.

BILLY

(*Weak smile*)
Well...uh...Colonel Ramm...

RAMM

You realize you're out of barracks without authority?

BILLY

Uh ... yes, sir.... (*Raises voice, trying to warn* DAN) Colonel
Ra-a-am. You see, Colonel ... (*Raises voice*) Ra-a-am ... You
see ... Colonel Ra-a-am ... (*Raises voice*) Colonel Ra-a-am ...

RAMM

Stop blustering, Mr. Randolph, and get back to barracks. Report yourself to the O.D. under arrest. I'll take care of this matter as soon as I return to town tomorrow.

BILLY

Yes, sir. (BILLY *exits meekly.* COLONEL RAMM *crosses to* CLAIRE.)

RAMM

Good night, Joyce. Sorry. (*He exits.* CLAIRE *meekly follows.*
Pause. JOYCE *makes sure that* COLONEL RAMM *has gone, then*
starts toward door. The upper section of the door opens and
DAN *appears. He looks off right.*)

JOYCE
(*With great relief*)
Well, thank heaven, Dan, you didn't get caught.

DAN

Thank heaven, my foot, thank the *walrus!*

Blackout

Curtain

ACT TWO

Scene II

Two-thirty P.M., the following day.
Scene: *Barracks room. Same as Act One, Scene I.*
The room is in total disorder. Off stage there is the sound of the VMI Alma Mater Song, being sung by cadets as they pass by the door. A general air of excitement exists. DAN *and* BING *are attired in baseball pants and stockings, are stripped to the waist. They are busy dressing for the game.*

The following words of the song can be heard as the boys pass by the door—some returning from Garrison Review—others on way to game. Shouts are heard from others as they pass by.

> *We love our old Alma Mater,*
> *True to alumnus and friend;*
> *As one we stand, throughout the land,*
> *Proud of our his'try and men;*
> *We love our old Alma Mater;*
> *We honor old V.M.I.*
> *It's the same in defeat or in vict'ry,*
> *For V.M.I. shall never die.*

A CADET
(Sticks head in door)
Give it to 'em in there, fellows. (*Disappears.*)

DAN
(Sitting on floor)
Now, listen, Bing. When that big Cavalier first baseman

comes to bat, I'll give you this one.... (*He assumes the position of a catcher, and illustrates signals*) You got it?

BING

Yeah...Low...on the outside corner...

DAN
(*Loud*)

Inside corner...*Inside* corner...

BING

O.K.

DAN

If you give him a high one, he'll murder it.

ANOTHER CADET
(*Enters exuberantly*)

Hey, Dan, my girl just got in from Sweetbriar. How would you like to have a date after the game? She brought along her roommate.

DAN
(*Pulling on a stocking*)

Thank you just the same, Alibi, but I'm up to my neck in roommates.

ANDREWS
(*Enters, pats* BING *on back*)

Well, pour it on 'em, fella. This is the day we've been waiting for.

(GRANT BOTTOME *enters, wearing a dress uniform, consisting of gray pants, coatee, white cross-belts across his chest, brass breast plate, white waist-belt with brass buckle, and bayonet hanging from belt. He runs and slides into room, assuming a "Finn-out" position: standing on his toes very stiffly, his chin tucked in, his shoulders strained back, with his forearms parallel to the floor.* BILLY *and* TOWNSEND *follow him. They also carry rifles, are wearing dress uniforms, with shakos on the back of their heads. All look hot and tired after a vigorous Garrison Review.*)

BILLY

Finn-out, Mistol! (BOTTOME *Finns-out.*)

ANDREWS

Come on, Alibi. (ANDREWS *and* CADET *exit.*)

BILLY

(*Angrily*)
You think my heels are a shoe rack, Mistol?

BOTTOME

I didn't know.

TOWNSEND

You didn't know *what?*

BOTTOME

I didn't know ... *sir* ...

TOWNSEND

Sound off ... (*During this barrage,* BING *and* DAN *continue to dress for game.* BILLY *puts his rifle in rack, unbuttons his coatee, and puts shako on table.*)

BOTTOME

(*Sounding off*)

Bottome, sir ... Wheeling, West Virginia, sir.

BILLY

Well, Finn-out ... some! (BOTTOME *strains harder to pull his chin in and his shoulders back*.)

TOWNSEND

(*Barks*)

And suck up your gut ... What's your rifle number, Mistol?

BOTTOME

971 ... 133, sir.

TOWNSEND

What's the quotation on the back of the parapet, Mistol?

BOTTOME

(*Quoting*)

"A group of honorable youths ... pressing up the hill of science ..." (DAN *gets up from floor and shoves* BOTTOME *out of the way as he crosses to basin*) Up the hill of science ... up the ... hill ...

BILLY

(*As he hangs his coatee in clothes compartment*)

Better shift into second, Mistol.

BOTTOME

Up the hill of science ... with ... noble emulation ... with noble ... I can't remember the rest of it, sir ...

BILLY

You can't *remember* ...

TOWNSEND
(*Loud*)

Can't *remember* ...

BILLY

You're the grossest, dumbest rat I ever saw around here. You *know* it?

BOTTOME

Yes, sir.

TOWNSEND

You know what you're in here for, doncha, Mistol?

BOTTOME

I think it's for stepping on Mr. Randolph's heels at Garrison Review, sir.

BILLY
(*Loud*)

You *think* ... Rats aren't supposed to *think* around here ... You *know* it?

BOTTOME

Yes, sir.

TOWNSEND

Then stop thinking.

BOTTOME

Yes, sir. (BILLY *crosses to clothes rack, gets a pile of soiled white gloves and cross-belts.*)

IIO

TOWNSEND

Who do you think you are—Tom Brown of Culver? This is no country club, Mistol.

BOTTOME

No, sir. (BILLY *crosses to* BOTTOME.)

BILLY

When you get out of here, you take these dikes around to your room, get 'em washed, and bring 'em back before you go to the ball game. You understand?

BOTTOME
(*Puts dikes in shako*)
Yes, sir.

BILLY

When you come back, bring your metal polish with you.

BOTTOME

Yes, sir.

BILLY
(*Points to* BING's *sabre in rack*)
You see that sabre, Mistol?

BOTTOME

Yes, sir.

BILLY

You better shine it so you can see your teeth in it. You know it?

BOTTOME

I know it, sir. (*He starts toward door.*)

III

BILLY

Hey, no one told you to go, Mistol Bottome. (BOTTOME *stops*)
Go over there and look in that mirror, and see how the grossest
rat in VMI looks. (BOTTOME *starts to cross to mirror.*)

BOTTOME

Yes, sir.

TOWNSEND

(*Pounding hand on table*)
Move, Mistol! (BOTTOME *jumps to mirror.*)

BILLY

Now give yourself pluperfect hell, Mistol.

BOTTOME

(*To mirror*)
Mistol Bottome, what in hell's a matter with you ... Mistol?
... You're gross. You're gross as hell. You *know* it ... You ...
haven't got enough brains to pour rain out of a boot.... Mistol
... You know it.... (*He stops for inspiration.*)

TOWNSEND

(*Looking at book*)
Keep goin'.

BOTTOME

(*To mirror*)
Yes, sir. You better stop thinking around here.... Don't you
know rats aren't supposed to think around here, Mistol? What
d' yuh think this is, Mistol ... Bill Jones of Culver ... or a
country club ... or something ... Mistol?

112

BILLY
(*Bored*)
Put some life into it.

TOWNSEND
(*Emphatic*)
Finn-out, Mistol!

BOTTOME
(*Jerking his shoulders back and taking* TOWNSEND'S *tone. To mirror*)
Finn-out, Mistol! You better snap to guard around here and watch where you're stepping at parade after this. Now put on your shako and get the hell out of here. Move! (*Before the others realize what he's done, he has exited.*)

TOWNSEND
(*Calling as he exits after* BOTTOME)
Hey, nobody told you to go. Wait a...

BILLY
(*Crosses to door*)
Well, I'll be damned! Nothing dumb about that rat. (BING *and* DAN *are completely dressed in baseball uniform.* BILLY *crosses to mirror and pats* BING *on back*) Now get in there with your whole heart and soul. Eat 'em up alive!

DAN
Don't get him excited.

BILLY
I'd sure like to be down there, but old Ramm-rod has made other plans for me. So I'll stay right in my little room praying for you.

BING

Thanks, Brother Rat. I'll do the best I know how. (*To* DAN)
Come on, Dan. Better get goin'... (*He starts toward door, as*
DAN *gathers up his shoes, gloves and cap.*)

BILLY
(*To* BING)

Don't forget, Bing. Give 'em the whole works. You'll never
know what it means to you. (*There is a sharp rap on door.*
All jump to attention. COLONEL RAMM *enters.*)

RAMM

Mr. Randolph!

BILLY

Yes, sir.

RAMM

You will be assigned your penalty, Monday. Until then you'll
remain in your room under arrest.

BILLY
(*Doleful*)

Yes, sir.

RAMM

Considering the short time before finals, Mr. Randolph, your
escapade of last night strikes me as being a mighty foolish act.

BILLY

Yes, sir.

RAMM

I deplore your lack of judgment in committing these flagrant
breaches of discipline.

114

BILLY

Yes, sir.

RAMM

You're a first-classman. You know better than to be out of barracks after taps.

BILLY

Well, sir ...

RAMM

The arrival of a few young ladies on the post is no signal for you to go out to entertain them.

BILLY

No, sir, but ...

RAMM
(*Restraining his impatience*)
What makes you do such unorthodox things, Mr. Randolph?

BILLY

Well, sir ... We only went up there ... to ...

RAMM

"*We?*" What did you say?

BILLY
(*Snared*)
I ... uh ... mean ... nothing, sir ...

RAMM
(*Slowly*)
Just a minute, here ... (BILLY *is dying*) Mr. Randolph, was there any cadet with you last night? (*No answer. Sternly*) Answer my question, Mr. Randolph.

BILLY

(*Licked, knowing he cannot lie to an officer*)
Yes, sir.

RAMM

(*Turns to* BING)
Mr. Edwards, were you out of barracks last night—without authority?

BING

No, sir. (*Pause.*)

RAMM

(*Turns to* DAN)
Were you, Mr. Crawford? (*Pause.*)

DAN

Sir, I don't have to answer that. It's a self-incriminating question.

RAMM

(*Grunts and turns to* BILLY)
Was Mr. Crawford with you last night?

BILLY

(*Hesitantly*)
Do I have to answer that, sir?

RAMM

(*He's had enough of this*)
It's not a self-incriminating question, is it?

BILLY

(*Weak*)
No ... sir ...

RAMM
(Threatening)

Then I'd advise you to answer it. Was he?

BILLY
(After a pause, weakly)

Yes, sir.

RAMM
(To DAN)

You will also remain in your room under arrest.

DAN
(Takes a step forward. Desperate)

But, sir ... the game ...

RAMM

You should have thought of that last night, Mr. Crawford.

DAN
(After a pause, weakly)

Yes, sir.

RAMM

First-classmen ... potential officers ... What am I running around here, a *country club?* (*Slams door behind him. There is a pause.*)

DAN
(Throws glove, shoes on floor)

Well, that's that. Better step off, Bing. (*Crosses to table*) Go ahead ... Hang in there. (BING *looks at* DAN *for a minute, then*

117

walks to door, turns, looks and tries to say something, but cannot.)

BING

(*Puts hand on his stomach, makes a helpless grimace*)
Yeah...But Dan...Gee...(*Exits. There is a pause.* DAN *looks at* BILLY *venomously.*)

BILLY

(*Quietly*)
Tough break...(DAN *just looks at him.* BILLY *sits on cot*)
We've got to do something. Let me think...

DAN

(*After having counted ten, sarcastically*)
Sure, you're the brains of the outfit. Let you do it...

BILLY

All right, I pulled a boner...I'm sorry...

DAN

You're always sorry.

BILLY

Who they going to get to take your place?

DAN

Aimee Semple McPherson. (*Slams chair on floor and sits at table.*)

BILLY

All right, Dan. Let's not be funny, boys. We might lose that game.

DAN

Go ahead. Think your way out of this one ... (*Derisively*) Brother Rat.

BILLY

I wouldn't care if it was *my* money ... But it's *his* money. Do you realize that guy has written two checks and there isn't a quarter in the bank? (*Gets another great idea*) Wait a minute ... I got an angle ... I'll fix it. Listen ... We bet all Bing's money on VMI, didn't we?

DAN

That's the second time today you've gotten all mixed up with the first person plural.

BILLY

All right, *I* bet the money.

DAN

That's better.

BILLY
(*Continuing*)

Bing is out there walking around in circles, isn't he?

DAN

Right. (*Starts biting his nails.*)

BILLY

There'll be a center fielder in there catching, won't there?

DAN

Right.

BILLY

You bat four hundred, don't you?

DAN

Right.

BILLY

And you'll be in here chewing on your fingernails?

DAN

Right. (*Tears fingers away from mouth.*)

BILLY

(*Summation*)

Which means that all the dough is going in the cesspool.

DAN

Now you got upstairs. Let's see you get down.

BILLY

O.K. Don't crowd me. Now. (*Leans over table, facing* DAN)
If we take the same amount of money ...

DAN

If we *had* the same amount of money.

BILLY

That's a technicality. If we took that same amount of money
and bet it on the other team ...

DAN

(*Bomb-shelled*)

The Cavaliers?

120

BILLY

Are you going to be a cheer leader?

DAN

But we...

BILLY

Then, when the game is over ... Where will we be?

DAN
(*Disgust*)

In the dog-house.

BILLY

We'll be *even*. D'yuh get it? *Even!* It's in the satchel. It's marvelous ... We can't miss ... (*Hurries to window and sticks head out, facing upward. Calls*) Window ... 411 ...

DAN

Get out o' that window, you idiot. You're under arrest.

BILLY
(*Ignores him*)

Window 4. Mr. Bottome. Come down here ... right away.

DAN

What do you want with him?

BILLY

He's going to do me a favor. (*Whistles and motions to* SLIM, *who is somewhere near barracks. Crosses to locker, takes out some money, and planks money down on table*) I've got a buck and a half.

DAN

Hoarding, eh? (*Gives in*) Well, I've got three dollars.

BILLY

Kick in. (DAN *takes money from drawer in table, and planks it down.* SLIM *enters through window and stands on window seat.*)

SLIM

What'll you have, Brother Rat?

BILLY

We're in an awful jam. You've got to help us out.

SLIM

Do anything I can.

BILLY

(*Slowly he crosses to* SLIM, *talking as he walks*)
Slim, how long we been Brother Rats?

SLIM

Four years.

BILLY

Been through a lot together, haven't **we**?

SLIM

Reckon we have.

BILLY

I never failed you in a pinch, did **I**?

SLIM

Can't say as you did, Brother Rat. (BILLY *shakes his hand fraternally.*)

BILLY

How much money you got?

SLIM

I was afraid of that.... Not very much. (*Slowly pulls out three dollars.*)

BILLY

(*Grabbing money*)

Three bucks! All right, Slim. How about this pocket?

SLIM

(*Hesitantly extricates five dollars from his jacket pocket*)

That's my eatin' money.

BILLY

Sorry, Slim. Hate to do it, but I've got to borrow it. (*Takes it out of* SLIM'S *hand*) Positively return it tomorrow morning.

SLIM

(*Kissing it good-bye with a look*)

O.K.

BILLY

Sure you haven't got any more?

SLIM

No, sir, Brother Rat. I had eight dollars more, but I bet it on VMI.

BILLY

All right, Slim. (BOTTOME *enters, Finns-out.*)

DAN

Sit down, Mistol. (BOTTOME *relaxes.*)

BILLY

(*Hands money to* DAN)
Throw it in the hotch-pot. (DAN *puts it with other money on table*) Now ... Have a chair, Mister Bottome.

BOTTOME

(*Amazed and uneasy*)

Yes, sir.

BILLY

(*Patronizingly*)
How would you like to do me a favor?

BOTTOME

Why ... uh ... all right, sir.

BILLY

Good. How much money you got?

BOTTOME

Sir?

BILLY

Money, you know—legal tender.

BOTTOME

Well, sir, I just got my monthly allowance from home.

DAN

How much is it? (*Slight pause, as they pray for right figure.*)

BOTTOME

Ten dollars.

BILLY

That's great, Mistol. I've got to borrow it.

BOTTOME
(*Swallowing*)

All right ... sir.

DAN
(*Sweetly*)

Can you get it now, Mistol?

BOTTOME

It's right here, sir. (*Reaches in blouse, pulls out envelope, blows it open, removes letter, to which is pinned a ten-dollar bill, and hands it to* BILLY.)

BILLY
(*After he takes money*)

You're an answer to a mother's prayer.

BOTTOME

Thank you, sir.

BILLY

Thank *you*, Mistol.

BOTTOME

Anything else, sir?

DAN

That's all for the time being.

BOTTOME

Yes, sir. (*Exits.*)

BILLY

(*Throws it on table*)
How much is that, Dan?

DAN

(*Counts money*)
Twenty-two-fifty. (*Short pause.*)

BILLY

(*Goes to locker, brings out little wooden box and takes out a pair of gold cuff links*)
Slim, how much would Barney give for these cuff links?

SLIM

In hock?

BILLY

Yeah.

SLIM

If they're gold, I reckon two dollars.

BILLY

Top?

SLIM

Top.

126

BILLY

(*Throws them to* DAN)

In the hotch-pot. (*Holds up cigarette case*) How 'bout this case?

SLIM

Buck ... Top!

BILLY

In the pot. Dan, write those down. (DAN *takes paper and writes.* BILLY *looks at watch*) Hate to do it. It was the old man's. (*Looks at* SLIM) Slim ...

SLIM

All watches is the same ... A fin ... (*Holds up hand.*)

BILLY

(*To* DAN)

I'll show you I mean business. (*Pause. Throws it in*) Dan ...

DAN

Yeah?

BILLY

You've got a watch.

DAN

(*Rises, pushes* SLIM *back, opens drawer, puts watch on table, slams drawer closed*)

I *had* a watch. (*Sits.*)

DAN

How about that medal?

BILLY

Yeah, the medal. (*Goes to locker and after throwing some of its contents on floor brings out gold medal*) How much, Slim?

SLIM

Buck.

BILLY

It's a *debating* medal.

SLIM

Buck and a half. (BILLY *tosses medal on table.* DAN *figures.*)

DAN

Thirty-seven dollars.

BILLY

Still shy thirteen.

SLIM

That's a bad number. (BILLY *stops, looks at* BING's *sabre, points to it.*)

DAN

(*Ominously*)

Get away from that sabre.

BILLY

(*Turns away*)

I was just thinkin'...

DAN

Get twenty years for what you're thinkin'.

128

SLIM

Standard price for class rings—five bucks...

BILLY

Barney's already got mine.

DAN

(*Takes off ring and throws it in pile*)

There's five more.

BILLY

We're still short. (*Points to books*) Slim, how about books?

SLIM

(*With finality*)

Ain't worth nuthin'.

BILLY

(*Crosses back to lockers. Stops, takes gold frame with picture from* BING's *locker*)

Slim, how much? Gold...

SLIM

Three dollars.

DAN

(*Touch of conscience*)

Not Bing's girl!

BILLY

Top?

SLIM

Top.

BILLY
(*Takes picture from frame*)
I hate to strip her. (*Puts frame in pile.*)

BILLY
What does that make it?

DAN
(*Figures*)
Forty-five dollars.

BILLY
Get a laundry bag, Dan. (DAN *gets laundry bag, empties contents, leaving pile of dirty laundry on floor near lockers.*)

BILLY
Have to hurry. Five dollars more. Where we gonna get five dollars? (*Looks toward sabre. Pause. Walks over to sabre and looks at it again*) Slim...

SLIM
Yeah... Brother Rat?

BILLY
(*Desperately takes down sabre*)
How much would it bring?

SLIM
(*Crosses to* BILLY)
That's United States Gover'ment property... Brother Rat...
I might go to Alcatraz.

BILLY
(*Impatient*)
Never mind that. Will it bring five bucks?

SLIM

(*Protesting*)

It'll bring five bucks, but I tell yuh...

BILLY

Bing won't need it till Monday. It's got to go. (*Holds out sabre to* SLIM.)

SLIM

(*Taking out handkerchief*)

Just a minute—no fingerprints. (*Grabs sabre with handkerchief.*)

BILLY

Come on, Dan. (*To* SLIM) How long will it take you to get over there and back? (BILLY *collects articles, puts money and articles and sabre in bag, and hands it to him.*)

SLIM

Five minutes.

BILLY

Make it four. Drive that crate like you never did in your life. Drop this load at Barney's, and then go out and bet this money...

SLIM

All...that...money?

BILLY

The whole bundle. All on the Cavaliers!

SLIM

(*Amazed*)

'Gainst VMI?

BILLY

Isn't strictly kosher. But it's got to be done.

SLIM

But, Brother Rat...I ain't never heard of a Keydet bettin' 'gainst VMI.

BILLY

(*Impatient*)

Good God, Slim, don't argue with me...get going. (SLIM *exits out window.*)

DAN

Make it fast. We'll be waiting for you.

BILLY

(*Cheers are heard off stage. Pause*)

How do those cheers sound to you, Dan—pro or con?

DAN

I don't know. (*Goes to window*) Wonder how Bing's doing.

BILLY

I'm afraid to think.

DAN

(*Sits on window seat*)

It's a tough one to miss. Never thought I'd be up here when our big game was being played. (*Both pause for a moment to think over their sins.* DAN *looks suspiciously at* BILLY) What are you doing, thinking again?

BILLY

Yeah.

DAN

Please don't. (*Looks away.*)

BILLY

I was just wondering how long old Ramm-rod is going to keep us incarcerated. (*Visualizing*) I can just picture the expression on my old man's face when he comes down here to see me graduate and finds I have to be led out of jail to get my diploma. If he wants to see me, he'll have to sit out there on the fence and I can wave to him through the window.

DAN

How 'bout my old man?

BILLY

I'll tell mine to push over and they can both sit on the fence. (MEMBER OF GUARD *enters, wearing blouse, white waist, belt with bayonet attached, and white gloves. Cheers from game.*)

MEMBER OF GUARD

Special for you, Randolph. (BILLY *takes letter.* MEMBER OF GUARD *exits.*)

BILLY

Here's my check. Damn it, why didn't it get here an hour sooner? (*He has opened letter. Looks for check, shakes envelope, but there is none enclosed. Reads letter.*)

DAN

Still love you?

BILLY

(*Scans letter. Reads aloud in a monotone*)
"I'm still enough of an optimist to await the day when I shall

receive a letter from you which does not contain an urgent request for an immediate remittance ..." (*Aside to* DAN) That's gratitude for you. (*Continues reading*) "I am sorry that I am unable to oblige. I do not control the United States Treasury, and they have stopped selling gold bricks on Broadway. I am only a normal business man, and there are others in the family besides you. One more year with you in college and we should all be raking leaves for the WPA."

DAN

A boy's best friend is his father. (BILLY *crumples letter and throws it on floor.*)

BILLY

You can't please that guy. (TOWNSEND *enters, excited. Cheers are heard.*)

TOWNSEND

Geez. It was horrible. I couldn't stand it. (*Crosses over to chair and falls into it, dramatizing his exhaustion.*)

BILLY

The game?

TOWNSEND

Oh, it's horrible.

DAN

Are we losing?

TOWNSEND

The Cavaliers scored eight runs in the first inning.

134

BILLY

Eight runs?

DAN

But, Bing...

TOWNSEND

Oh, it was horrible.

DAN

Did they get eight runs off Bing in the first inning?

TOWNSEND

He walked the first four men... Then that Cavalier first baseman got a home run.... Before we could eat another peanut, they had three more....

DAN

I knew it...

TOWNSEND
(Describing)

Dan, I never saw him like that before. He was out there in a fog...

BILLY
(Sitting on cot)

Guess he couldn't get started.

TOWNSEND

And then it happened...

DAN
(Alarmed)

What happened?

135

TOWNSEND

A guy got up and hit a line drive, and Bing just stood there.
I swear ... The ball bounced from his head to the dugout.

DAN

Is he hurt?

TOWNSEND

Gee, I don't know. He fell down ...

BILLY

Where is he now?

TOWNSEND

They carried him to the dressing room ...

BILLY

(*Concerned. Rises and starts pushing* TOWNSEND *out*)
Go down and find out how he is.

TOWNSEND

It must have taken ten years off my life. Geez, it was horrible.
(*Exits.* SLIM *has been climbing in the window. He is excited.*)

SLIM

Sorry, Brother Rat. Couldn't lay that bet ... too late....

BILLY

(*Mortified*)

Too late?

SLIM

(*Out of breath*)

Game had started.

136

DAN

Holy ... How about the stuff?

SLIM

Here's your pawn ticket, and here's the money—all except the eight dollars and fifty cents for the two trips. (*Hands money and ticket to* DAN. *Keeps eight dollars.*)

BILLY

(*To* SLIM)

You picked a helluva time to fail me.

SLIM

Certify ... Brother Rat ... Did the best I could. Anything else I can do?

DAN

Rush down to the game and find out what they're doing.... (SLIM *exits out window as* BING *enters in a daze. He has a bandage on his forehead. He is carrying his baseball shoes.* DAN *rushes to* BING, *and leads him to table.*)

DAN

Bing, you all right?

BING

Just a little dizzy.

BILLY

C'mon, Bing, sit down.

DAN

Take it easy, Bing.

BING

(*Sits*)

Gawd, it was like a nightmare. (*Cheers are heard.* BILLY *starts to examine* BING's *head.*)

BILLY

How's the head?

BING

(*Rubbing his head*)

Gee, I don't know.

BILLY

Can I get you something?

BING

No...I mean...I reckon...no....

BILLY

How about some water? (*Starts for basin.*)

DAN

(*To* BILLY)

Leave him alone. He's all right.

BILLY

What was the matter with you, Bing? Why didn't you duck?

BING

I was thinkin' 'a Kate.

DAN

(*Disgust*)

Women!

138

BILLY

Look, I'm thinking of Kate. (*Bends his body forward as if he were ducking*) I can duck! (BING *waves arm at* BILLY. *Mournfully*) Eight runs...

DAN

With or without me, you can do better than that.

BING
(*Entreatingly*)

How can a fella pitch... when he's havin' a baby? (SLIM *rushes up and talks excitedly through window.*)

SLIM

I told yuh, Brother Rat... we're headin' for trouble.

BILLY
(*Jumps up*)

Trouble?

SLIM

Commandant just stopped me.

DAN

Commandant?

BILLY

What'd he want?

SLIM

He put the thumb screws on me. Knows about the sabre....
(BILLY *tries to shush* SLIM.)

DAN

Good God!

SLIM

Barney Marcus went chicken. Called up old Ramm, and gave
'im the serial number.

DAN

Serial number!

BILLY
(*Starts pacing*)
I gotta think. (TOWNSEND *enters hurriedly from doorway, as*
SLIM *disappears*.)

TOWNSEND

The game looks awful black. (BING *sits up*.)

BING

How're we doin'?

BILLY

Scram, Townsend, powder....

BING

Any chance of winnin'?

TOWNSEND

Not a chance in the world. But Harrington's pitching a great
game.

BILLY

Bounce out of here, Townsend. Got no time for ball games.
(BOTTOME *enters carrying laundry bag.* BILLY *shouts at top of his
voice*) What the hell do you want, Mistol?

140

TOWNSEND

Yeah!

BOTTOME

(*Scared to death*)

But ... sir ... I ... uh ... just ...

BILLY

(*Impatient*)

Get the hell outta here! Doncha see we're busy?

BOTTOME

But, sir, you told me to come down to shine Mr. Edwards' sabre. (BING *hears his name mentioned, and "sabre" registers for the first time.*)

BING

Sabre?

BILLY

Good God, Mistol, didn't you hear me? (*A sharp rap is heard on glass of door and* COLONEL RAMM *strides into the room. Bedlam is loose, the room having become more and more in disorder. All jump to attention.* COLONEL RAMM *makes hurried survey of room, and crosses to* BOTTOME.)

RAMM

What are you doing in here?

BOTTOME

(*Frightened*)

Well ... I ... uh ...

RAMM
(*Sternly*)
Who told you to come down here?

BOTTOME
(*Innocently*)
Well ... sir ... I only came down to shine Mr. Edwards' sabre.

RAMM
(*Crosses to* EDWARDS)
Shine his sabre! (*To* BOTTOME) Drive on to your room.

BOTTOME
Yes, sir. (*Exits.*)

RAMM
(*To* BING, *sternly*)
So you haze new cadets, too? (BING *is speechless*) As well as writing checks without funds. ...

BING
But, sir ... I didn't ...

RAMM
You're not going to stand there and deny that you wrote a check for twelve dollars to Dr. Kimball?

BING
I did, sir ... but ... I ...

RAMM
(*Sarcastic*)
But you were going to deposit the money. What's the serial number of your sabre? (*He looks at slip of paper.*)

BING

113 ... 724 ... sir.

RAMM

I thought so. Well, you won't need a sabre any more, Mr. Edwards.

BILLY

But Colonel Ramm, I want to tell you ...

RAMM
(*Loudly*)
I'm not addressing you, Mr. Randolph.

BING

But, sir ...

RAMM
(*To* BING)
You're under arrest. Monday morning you will answer to me for hazing a new cadet, writing a check without funds, and pawning United States Government property. (*Enraged he starts toward door, stops, turns*) Who's the orderly of this disgraceful room?

BING
(*Helplessly*)
I am, sir....

RAMM

And add to that report: Room in gross disorder. (*He storms out of room.* BING *in daze, sinks into chair, sits with head in hands.* DAN *turns, looking daggers at* BILLY, *comes down beside him.*)

143

DAN

Now I hope you're satisfied, you stupid maniac. I told you ...

BILLY

All right, all right. You said you thought we'd win the game. Why didn't you ...

DAN

Betting his dough, dragging me out in the middle of the night ...

BILLY

Now, wait a minute.

DAN

And having me put under arrest. How could Bing ...

BILLY

How the hell did I know we were going to get caught, we took a chance. ...

DAN

Why don't you take the chances and stop involving other people?

BILLY

Involving other people? What do you mean involving other ...

DAN

Betting Bing's money and ...

BILLY

Who bet it?

DAN

Who bet it? You bet it. And hocking everything we own. (*The following dialogue is delivered simultaneously and builds to a crescendo.*)

DAN

How about that sabre? He wouldn't need it until Monday. You hollow brain! You might have known that Barney would call the Commandant. Somebody ought to take that empty squash of yours and punch it full of holes. You haven't enough brains...

BILLY

Now, wait a minute. I'm not going to stand here and take the rap for all the hocking. You were in it just as deep as I was. How was I supposed to know Barney Marcus wasn't honest? Don't stand there and bellyache to me. Yeah, we...
(BILLY *and* DAN *are shouting at each other*)

BING

(*Cues in on* BILLY's *line* "Barney Marcus wasn't honest")
Quiet! (BILLY *and* DAN *stop abruptly. A pause. Naïvely*) You want to get us into trouble?

Curtain

ACT THREE

ACT THREE

Scene I

Two months later. 10:30 P.M., two nights before commencement.

Scene: *In front of barracks. One wall of barracks commences about a third of the way upstage and extends about eight feet at a forty-five-degree angle toward the audience, where it rounds out into a tower room, completes a semicircle, and projects upstage on a diagonal to a point one-third the distance from back wall of stage, where it again rounds out into a tower room and continues in a straight line until it meets the main arch of barracks upstage. The wall of barracks continues from the arch to the back wall of the stage. In this diagonal of barracks are three rows of lighted windows opening offstage. Also three windows, one above the other in tower rooms. There is a small illuminated light bulb on a metal arm at the top of the main arch. There is a stone parapet and fence extending from back wall along left side of the stage. A French cannon of the Napoleonic period is mounted right of parapet. It is encircled by a large iron chain.*

BING, BILLY *and* DAN, *rifles on shoulders, are walking penalty tours. They are dressed in white summer penalty tour uniform, consisting of white duck trousers, white shirts, white waist belts with brass buckles, bayonets hanging from belts, black cartridge boxes on back of belts, black ties and gray cadet caps. They are walking in single file, slowly, back and forth across the stage.)*

DAN

(*Continuing an argument*)

Well, you're all wrong, and I'll tell you why. The days of the rugged individualist are over. Look at the WPA. Look at relief.

BILLY

(*Positive*)

Do you want to know what put us on the relief rolls? I'll tell you what—the World War! (*The talk begins quietly, and gradually increases in volume.*)

DAN

(*Disgusted*)

The World War!

BILLY

All right now, you know so much about it. I'll tell you *how*. A bunch of crack-pots gathered around a table in a saloon in Europe and sold Uncle Sam an idea. So what do we do? We send all our raw materials, all our resources, all our assets over there to make the world safe for democracy.

DAN

(*Faces* BILLY)

Who sent them over?

BILLY

Who the hell do you think sent them over?

DAN

The rugged individualists.

150

BILLY

Congress, that's who....

DAN

Yeah, and who controlled Congress? The rugged individual-
.sts. That's who controlled Congress.

BILLY

(*Cornered*)

Now you're talking like a Louisiana Democrat. You haven't
the remotest conception of the problem, or ...

DAN

No?

BILLY

No. And you haven't the faintest idea of the meaning of
rugged individualism. Just because ... (*The volume of their
voices increases.* BING, *crossing back to them, waves his hand,
telling them to quiet down.*)

BING

You two better settle down or the O.D.'ll be out here and
bone the three of us. (*All three start marching, and as they turn,
a bugle is heard, blowing call to quarters. There is a pause in
dialogue until call is over.*)

BILLY

(*Keeps his voice lower*)

Funny how the last tour is always the longest.

DAN

How many more have you got, Bing?

151

BING

Three.

BILLY

You'll be able to finish them up tomorrow afternoon. (BILLY *and* DAN *continue left.* BING *turns and stands under light, over arch. He leans on rifle.*)

BING

I don't reckon there'll be much use walkin' 'em tomorrow, after I bull that chemistry exam in the morning.

BILLY

Why not?

BING

I'm not like you fellows. I have to study to get my subjects. I should be in there now poundin' 'em. They piled up so many penalty tours on me, I haven't had fifteen minutes to myself in the last two months.

BILLY

Oh, you'll pass. (*Slight pause. The boys are tired.*)

BING
(*Quietly*)

Kate's in the hospital.

DAN
(*Stops right of* BING)

Is she, Bing?

BILLY

How's she doing?

152

BING

Like they all do, I reckon.

BILLY

When do they expect it?

BING

The baby?

BILLY

Yeah.

BING
(*Confused*)

Well, she had to go to the hospital.... This baby business ... I'm not so good at that....

BILLY

I don't know. You're doing all right.

DAN

Well, don't worry about it, Bing.

BILLY
(*Crossing down right*)

Hell, no. Having a baby these days is no worse than a bad cold. What with all the scientific progress nowadays, women go to bed at night and wake up in the morning with a baby and they haven't the least idea where it came from. (*The boys have gradually worked their way to the right corner of barracks.* BILLY *stands down right.* BING *and* DAN *continue to walk.*)

153

BILLY

(*Looking off right and leaning on rifle*)

Gee, that's a pretty moon.

DAN

Lay off the moon. (BING *and* DAN *continue walking*) That's why we're out here!

BILLY

(*Looking off*)

The lights are still on in the Commandant's house.

DAN

Hope the chandelier falls off and lands on his think tank.

BILLY

He wouldn't even feel it. (*Pause.* DAN, *followed by* BING, *turns and walks right*) I wonder what that old buzzard does over there every night?

DAN

Well, he's married. . . .

BILLY

To a four-star Tobe.

BING

Mrs. Ramm's a nice lady.

BILLY

Ever see her?

BING

Sure.

154

DAN

Got a face like a gargoyle.

BILLY

Well, he probably covers her face with a worn-out flag and loves her for old glory. (ANDREWS *pokes his head out of window near arch.*)

ANDREWS

Hey, Billy! Dan! O.D. coming through the arch. (BILLY, DAN *and* BING *start to walk tours in single file, in regulation fashion.* HARRINGTON *as Officer of the Day enters from arch. He is dressed in white-duck trousers, gray blouse, gray cap, red sash, officer's black leather waist belt, sabre, wears white gloves.*)

HARRINGTON
(*With authority*)

Break it up over there. (BILLY, DAN *and* BING *cross, turn, and start back*) Break it up. This is not a sewing circle. You're walking penalty tours. (*The three boys walk in single file*) There's two ways to do a thing around here, the right way and the wrong way. You can always depend upon you three to do it the wrong way. (HARRINGTON *is standing officiously to the right of arch.*)

BILLY
(*Ragging him*)

Mr. O.D.? (BILLY, DAN *and* BING *stop, facing* HARRINGTON.)

HARRINGTON

What is it?

BILLY

Do you approve of the way I'm carrying my butt?

HARRINGTON

Your what?

BILLY
(*Points to the butt of his rifle*)

My butt.

HARRINGTON

All right, Randolph, keep that up and I'll bone you. And when you address the O.D., put a sir on it.

BILLY

Yes, sir.

DAN

How much time left, Mr. O.D.?

HARRINGTON
(*Every inch a soldier*)

I'll dismiss you when your tour is over.

DAN

Thank you.

BILLY
(BILLY *turns head, prompting him*)

Sir ... sir ...

DAN

Thank you, sir.

BILLY
(*Still ragging* HARRINGTON)

Sir ... Mr. O.D., sir. May I ask a question of the Mr. O.D., sir?

HARRINGTON

You can get moving and be damn quick about it. Get funny with me, and see where you wind up. (HARRINGTON *exits through arch.* BILLY, DAN *and* BING *start walking, and as they make turn, off-stage voices are heard shouting: "Turkey! Turkey! Turkey!"*)

BILLY

Women, Women! (*A* CADET *appears in window on second floor of barracks and yells.*)

A CADET

Turkey! Turkey! (*Voices off stage, "Turkey!" Calls in barracks of "Turkey."* HARRINGTON *enters through arch. Cries cease. The* CADET *disappears.*)

HARRINGTON
(*Calling*)

Window 217! (*No one appears*) Come to the window, 217. (*The* CADET *appears in window*) Were you standing in the window just now?

ANDREWS

Yes, sir.

HARRINGTON

Cut out that hollering, and stay out of that window or I'll bone you again. (HARRINGTON *writes on slip of paper.*)

A CADET
(*Forlornly from window*)

Yes, sir. (*Disappears.* JOYCE *and* CLAIRE, *dressed in summer clothes, enter.* BILLY, *unable to talk in the presence of the O.D.,*

157

signals greetings to the girls. HARRINGTON *crosses to* JOYCE *and*
CLAIRE.)

HARRINGTON

Hello, girls. When did you get in, Joyce?

JOYCE

This afternoon.

HARRINGTON
(Shaking hands)

Good evening, Miss Ramm.

CLAIRE

What were you doing just now?

HARRINGTON
(Official)

Just my duty.

CLAIRE

Did he do anything wrong?

HARRINGTON

He did, and I'll have to report him. Two nights before commencement is no time to let up on discipline. (*The boys continue to walk tours in silence.* HARRINGTON *talks to girls as the boys walk slowly on.*)

JOYCE

It was just sweet of you, Harley, to ask me down for Finals. I could hardly wait for school to be over to get here.

158

HARRINGTON

I knew you'd want to be here to see me graduate.

JOYCE

Did you get through all your exams all right?

HARRINGTON

Well, I have chemistry tomorrow morning, but I won't have any trouble with that.

CLAIRE

(*Looking at boys*)

Gee, don't they look cute marching? (*The boys are crossing left and are in sight*) Let's go over and talk to them. (CLAIRE *crosses a few steps and stops.*)

HARRINGTON

(*Stopping her*)

They're not allowed to talk to anyone.

JOYCE

No, Claire. They're walking penalty tours.

CLAIRE

What did they do?

JOYCE

Why, Claire.... (JOYCE *and* HARRINGTON *just look at her.*)

CLAIRE

(*Recalls*)

Oh ...

JOYCE

(*Crosses to* CLAIRE *and takes her hand*)

Well, Claire, I guess we'd better be getting back.

159

HARRINGTON

I'm afraid I'll have to leave you.

JOYCE

'Bye, Harley, we'll see you tomorrow.

HARRINGTON

Good night. (HARRINGTON *bows.*)

CLAIRE

(*Kidding as she exits around side of barrack*)
Keep everything under control, Mister O.D.

HARRINGTON

That's what I'm here for. 'Bye.... (JOYCE *exits with* CLAIRE.
HARRINGTON *starts toward arch. To the boys*) All right...Keep
it moving out here.... Just because your tours are almost over,
that's no reason to stall.

BILLY

(*As* HARRINGTON *exits*)
That's what I'm here for, sir.

DAN

And a little boy shall lead them.

BILLY

(*With derision*)
See him shine his tail in front of Joyce? (*Still derisively*) All
his life he'll be marching to the men's room to the tune of "The
Stars and Stripes Forever." (CLAIRE *has stealthily re-entered.*
JOYCE *follows a few feet behind. The girls stand watching the
boys and laugh quietly.*)

160

CLAIRE
(*Quietly*)

Dan. (DAN *continues to walk toward girls.*)

DAN
(*Dispassionately*)

Hello. (*Continues to walk tour.* BILLY *pauses as he turns.*)

BILLY

Hello, Joyce. How are you? Gee, you look gorgeous, even on penalty tours. (*Looks toward arch to see if* HARRINGTON *is in sight.*)

JOYCE
(*Waves to* BILLY)

Hello, Billy.

CLAIRE

How are you, Billy? (BILLY *stops walking at center.*)

BILLY

Feet are tired, but my heart is pure. (DAN *continues to walk back and forth. To* JOYCE) I'll be through with tours in a few minutes, and I'm coming right over to see you.

JOYCE
(*As she crosses, to* BILLY)

No you're not, Billy Randolph.

CLAIRE
(*To* DAN)

Dan, I want to tell you something.

DAN

All right, but I can't stop walking.

CLAIRE

Billy stopped. Why can't you? (DAN *makes turn and starts to cross.*)

DAN

'Cause when he stops, sane people walk. (CLAIRE *gets around in front of* DAN, *walks backward, in step with him.*)

BILLY
(*To* JOYCE)

Oh, I see. You framc me so you can have a clear field with that war-winner, Harrington.

JOYCE

Now stop that drivel. You know that I only came down here on his bid because you were under confinement.

BILLY

I'll be out from under confinement tomorrow night.

CLAIRE
(*Walking with* DAN)

Why didn't you answer my letter?

DAN
(*As he turns*)

I'm not very good at it. (BILLY *and* JOYCE *talk quietly.*)

CLAIRE

I want to apologize for getting you into all this trouble.

162

DAN

Forget it. If it hadn't been you, it would have been something else. (DAN *turns and stops under light over arch*) God blessed me with a roommate.

BILLY

(*To* JOYCE)

Well, I'll be down there after taps. And if you don't like it, call the Commandant.

JOYCE

Oh, Billy ... You're impossible. (BING *is walking toward right side of stage.*)

BILLY

(*Calling to* BING)

Bing, come here.... (BING *joins* BILLY *and* JOYCE.)

DAN

(*Standing with* CLAIRE *under light*)

Oh, it was just another ball game, but it meant a lot to Bing. ... And he's having such a lousy time....

CLAIRE

Hello, Bing.

BING

Hello, Claire. (*They have stopped walking.* DAN *and* CLAIRE *cross to* BILLY, JOYCE *and* BING.)

JOYCE

How are you, Bing? It's good to see you.

BING

(*To* JOYCE)

I'm mighty grateful to you, Joyce, for lending me that money.

JOYCE

That's all right, Bing. I was mighty pleased to have the chance to help you and Kate.

BING

I don't know how I would have been able to cover those checks. If you hadn't come to my rescue, I would have been shipped.

JOYCE

Oh, don't mention it, Bing.

BILLY

What do you think would have happened to me? Instead of walking penalty tours, I'd be selling gardenias in a subway station.

JOYCE

Oh, I was glad to do it, Billy.

BILLY

(*Looking down at rifle*)

I suppose I'll have to marry you now, so you can regain your self-respect.

CLAIRE

(*Quietly*)

Oh, there must be some other way.

JOYCE

The money wouldn't have done any good if Claire hadn't pleaded with her father to let me do it.

BILLY

It's great to have a drag with the United States Army.

BING

Wish I could pay you back now, but ...

BILLY

Don't worry, Joyce. Bing's gonna have a fortune.

CLAIRE

When, Bing?

BILLY

Soon as he graduates and wins the Athletic Award.

BING

(*Disconsolately*)

Doesn't look like I'm goin' to win the Award or graduate.

JOYCE

Why, Bing, I'm surprised to hear you talk like that.

CLAIRE

Of course you're going to graduate.

BING

(*Shaking head*)

'Fraid I ain't.

DAN

Bing has his toughest exam tomorrow, and he hasn't had time to crack a book.

JOYCE

What is it?

BING

Chemistry.

CLAIRE

You can certainly pass chemistry.

BILLY
(*Too sure*)

Sure you can.

BING
(*Discouraged*)

'Fraid it's gonna throw me.

CLAIRE

Why, Bing Edwards, I'm surprised to hear you talk like that. I could teach you enough chemistry in three hours to make you pass any exam they gave around this place.

BILLY
(*Getting great idea*)

Wait a minute. (*Crosses slowly to* CLAIRE) Did you really mean that? Three hours, Claire?

CLAIRE

Easy. I could spot the questions.

166

BILLY

Have you got any guts?

CLAIRE

Well, I'm the Commandant's daughter.

DAN

(*Leaning on rifle*)

True...but untimely.

BILLY

(*Excited again*)

O.K. You're elected. We'll smuggle you into barracks. You can spot the exam for Bing.

DAN

(*Loudly*)

I certify the guy has *dementia præcox*.

CLAIRE

(*Liking the idea*)

I'll do it. When do we start?

BILLY

Right away. (*Takes quick look for O.D.*) You get in our room now. We'll be through with our tours in a couple of minutes. (BILLY *takes* CLAIRE *by the hand and pulls her toward window in tower.* JOYCE *takes her other hand and pulls her back.* BILLY *pulls her to window again.*)

JOYCE

For God's sake, Claire, be careful!

BILLY

It's perfectly safe.

JOYCE

You boys are crazy. You can't do this. (*The boys glance toward arch.*)

BILLY

It's perfectly safe. I figured it all out. (DAN *and* BING *look at each other*) It's in the bag. Here you go. (BILLY *helps* CLAIRE *to window. She turns facing audience.*)

DAN

Wait a minute. (*To* CLAIRE) Listen, Claire, are you sure you want to do it?

CLAIRE

Of course I do.

DAN

But if your father ...

CLAIRE

I'm not afraid of the Commandant.

BILLY

Of course not.... Keep under cover till we get there.

JOYCE

Suppose they find you ...

ANDREWS

Hey! O.D. coming through the courtyard. Better get moving, you dopes.

168

BILLY
(*Pushing* JOYCE *off*)
Beat it, Joyce, I'll see you later.

JOYCE
But, Claire...

BILLY
She's all right. I'll be over and see you after taps. Get out.
(*Pushing* CLAIRE *farther into the room*) Get back out of sight.
(JOYCE *exits.* BILLY *starts walking very fast, back and forth, and overtakes* DAN *and* BING, *who are walking in a normal fashion.*)

DAN
(*To* BILLY *as he comes toward them*)
Aren't you overdoing it? (HARRINGTON *and a* MEMBER OF THE GUARD *enter from arch.* BILLY, BING *and* DAN *are walking in a military manner, when* HARRINGTON *and* GUARD *appear.*)

HARRINGTON
(*Standing with* GUARD, *facing backs of* BILLY, DAN *and* BING, *who are crossing right*)
Halt the tours!

MEMBER OF GUARD
(*Commands*)
Penalty tours, halt! Fall in. (*The three boys halt, come to order arms and stand abreast of each other, facing* GUARD *and* HARRINGTON.)

HARRINGTON
(*Commands*)
Call the roll!

MEMBER OF GUARD

(*Reading from tour sheet*)

Edwards.

BING

Here, sir.

MEMBER OF GUARD

Crawford.

DAN

Here, sir.

MEMBER OF GUARD

Randolph.

BILLY

Here, sir. (GUARD *turns to* HARRINGTON *and salutes.* HARRINGTON *returns the salute.*)

MEMBER OF GUARD

All present and accounted for, sir.

HARRINGTON

(*To* BILLY, BING *and* DAN)

I suppose I oughta congratulate you three for not trying to put anything over on me tonight. (*Louder*) Dismissed!

(HARRINGTON *and* GUARD *cross to left,* HARRINGTON *writes on paper.* BING *crosses to arch as* CLAIRE *appears in window.* DAN *motions to her to get back and* BILLY *swaggers out, as the curtain falls.*)

ACT THREE

Scene II

About two hours later, that night.

Scene: *Barracks room, same as Act I, Scene 2. There are blankets hanging over window and over the door to prevent the light in the room from being visible outside. There is a cot made up and ready for use, another cot, and a third, a short distance left of table. The table is strewn with books and papers.*

BOTTOME, *dressed in white pants and gray blouse, is standing at the door looking through a peep-hole in the blanket.* DAN, *wearing white pants and a polo shirt, is dozing on a cot.* BING *in white pants and a red sweat shirt is sitting at the table facing audience, working diligently over a problem.* CLAIRE *is helping* BING.

CLAIRE

(*To* BING, *as he starts throwing sheet away*)
What's the matter with that?

BING

It's wrong.

CLAIRE

No, it isn't.

BING

What do you mean, it isn't? I get two reactions.

CLAIRE

You're trying to find out what products if any are formed, aren't you?

171

BING

Yeah, but the creosol reacts with the sulphuric acid and gives you phenol *sulphonic* acid. (*He turns to page in book*) And here, in another reaction, it gives you phenol *sulphuric* acid.

CLAIRE

But you have acetic acid as a catalyst. (*She turns to another page in book*) Look here. (*Reads*) "Unlike alcohol, phenol does not form an acetate when heated with acetic acid even in the presence of an acid as a catalyst."

BING

Well, then no products are formed. (BOTTOME *moves around chair, straddles it and peers through hole.*)

CLAIRE

That's the answer. No products are formed. (*Turns to page in book*) Now work this one.

BING

O.K. (*Starts to work on problem.* CLAIRE *crosses to cot and runs her hand over* DAN'S *face.*)

DAN

(*Drowsily*)

Cut it out. (CLAIRE *tickles him again*) Goddammit...I'll... (CLAIRE *laughs.* DAN *lifts head, sees* CLAIRE. *Embarrassed*) Oh, s'cuse me. I suppose you've got to expect anything in a co-ed school. (*There is a knock at the window.*)

DAN

(*Startled at knock, then relaxes*)

That's Slim ... Douse 'em. (DAN *jumps off cot.* BOTTOME *turns out the light.* DAN *crosses to window, lifts blanket*) Thanks, Slim

.. O.K., turn 'em on. Bing ... (BING *turns on light.* DAN *crosses* *o cot with large paper bag*) Here's the good old scorf. (*Starts* *'o take out containers of Coca-Cola and sandwiches from bag,* *'uts them on the cot. Gives one to* CLAIRE, *who sits down beside* *him.*)

CLAIRE

Thanks. This night work sure makes a guy hungry. (*She* *'urns to* BOTTOME) Come and get it, Mr. Brother-Rat Bottome.

BOTTOME
(*Hesitantly*)

Yes, sir. (*Looks at* DAN.)

DAN
(*Good-naturedly*)

Come on, Mistol.

BOTTOME

(*Smiling, crosses to cot. He reaches out hand for sandwich*) Coming, sir.

CLAIRE

Wait a minute. (*She's learning*) Finn-out some! (CLAIRE *rises,* *puts sandwich in* BOTTOME's *mouth, who starts to cough. Sand-* *wich hangs from mouth as he stands in Finn-out position.*) Sit down, Mistol.

BOTTOME
(*Slowly returns to chair*)

Thank you, sir.

CLAIRE
(*Brings sandwich to* BING)

How's it coming, Bingo?

BING

Aw gee, I ain't goin' to pass that exam.

CLAIRE

Bing!

BING

(*Throws pencil down in disgust*)

No use, Claire... I'm mighty 'preciative of you wastin' al
this time and spottin' these questions for me, but it's no use
You can't get apples out of an empty barrel.

CLAIRE

You got the rest of 'em all right.

BING

Yeah, I know... But my brain just ain't proportionate to th
carbon cycle.

DAN

Now you're just working yourself up into a storm.

CLAIRE

(*Pushing him back in chair*)

Now you listen to me, Bing Edwards. (*Puts her hands on hi
shoulders. Sails into him*) I'm tired of listening to you talk lik
an anemic schoolboy. You ought to be ashamed of yourself. Al
you have left to learn are one or two problems and you'll knock
that exam cold.

BING

Yeah, but...

CLAIRE

Yeah, but ... You only need a seventy-nine to pass this course and you sit there wasting your evening worrying about it instead of doing what you're told. You think I'm over here because I like the night air ...

BING

Aw, Claire ... Don't get mad. I 'preciate all you're ...

CLAIRE
(Feigned anger)

Appreciate my Aunt Susie ... Save your *cheers* till after the game. Now get to work and crack that problem. (BING *returns to work*) And don't let me hear another peep out of you until it's finished. (*Starts away from table*) You'd think you had to work out the Theory of Relativity. (BING *looks up for a moment, then, almost afraid of her, starts to work industriously.*)

DAN
(Hands on hips)

Boy, what a blast! (CLAIRE *removes her glasses and brushes her hair back from her face.*)

CLAIRE

That's what you need around here—a little discipline. (*She starts to pull blanket and peek out window.*)

DAN

Hey, don't touch that blanket ... (CLAIRE *pulls hand away from blanket and crosses to mirror*) Or we will be in trouble. (*Pause as* CLAIRE *turns from mirror and starts to put on glasses again*) Hey, why don't you leave them off for a while? (DAN *sits.*)

CLAIRE

What?

DAN

The blinkers.

CLAIRE

Oh, maybe I will.

DAN

(*With his mouth full*)
Makes you look less like a bacteriologist.

CLAIRE

Yes, but "men never make passes at girls who wear glasses."

DAN

When you were traveling incognito, that wasn't such a problem.

CLAIRE

That's right, but ... Adams doesn't live here any more. (*Crosses to rifle rack and puts hand on one of the rifles.* BING *continues to study*) Say, Dan, if the Commandant caught me, would I have to join the penalty tours?

DAN

No, but I'd have to join the French Foreign Legion. (CLAIRE *takes rifle off rack and puts it on her shoulder. Crosses and turns at mirror.*)

CLAIRE

How would I look walking penalty tours, Brother-Rat Crawford?

176

DAN

You're no brother-rat of mine.

CLAIRE

Why, you ungrateful ...

DAN

(*Good-naturedly*)

Imagine being a brother-rat of anyone in the Ramm family.

CLAIRE

I see ... You're going to draw the color line. (CLAIRE *tries to execute order arms, but the result is awkward. Butt of rifle lands loudly on floor.*)

DAN

Look out, it'll fall on your toes.

CLAIRE

Well, show me the right way.

DAN

That's no fun at one o'clock in the morning.

CLAIRE

It is for me. Come on. (*Strikes military attitude.*)

DAN

(*Gives command from cot*)

Port ... ARMS! (CLAIRE, *in her inimitable way, executes port arms, holding rifle wrong*) No, that's wrong. Here ... (DAN *rises, crosses to* CLAIRE, *and takes rifle from her*) Watch me. (*Stands at attention with rifle butt resting on floor*) Port ... ARMS! (DAN *executes port arms.*)

CLAIRE

Oh, I see.

DAN

Now you try it. (CLAIRE *takes rifle and stands at order arms*) Port ... ARMS! (CLAIRE *executes port arms, but instead of rifle being on a diagonal, it is parallel to floor.* DAN *gets around in back of her*) Now watch my hands. (*He encircles her waist and, trying to cover her hands on rifle, he misses and puts his hand on* CLAIRE'S *stomach.*)

CLAIRE
(*Drops rifle butt to floor*)

I will.

BING

Cut out the noise, Dan, they'll hear you all over barracks. (DAN *steps away from her. Faces her.*)

DAN

Now ... Order ARMS! (CLAIRE *brings rifle down with a bang.* BING *is finding it quite impossible to study.* DAN *dashes to window and looks out*) Hey ... easy ... all right ... Port ... ARMS! (CLAIRE *executes port arms.*)

CLAIRE
(*Smiling*)

That's the one I like.

DAN

Order ... ARMS!

BOTTOME
(*From door, excited*)

Officer coming up the stoop with a flashlight.

DAN

Turn 'em off, Bing. (*Calls out*) Take your posts! (BING *turns out the light. There is a scuffle in the dark, as* BOTTOME *and* DAN *pull down the blankets, and all four take their posts. After a short pause all are quiet, except* DAN *mumbling incoherently. The light of a flashlight appears in door and an* OFFICER *enters. He walks to table, and turns on the light. It is* COLONEL RAMM. *He looks about the room, almost sniffs the air, and glances over the three occupied cots. The covers are drawn over the heads of two of the occupants.* DAN *continues, supposedly in his sleep*) Port...ARMS...right should...order ARMS...(COLONEL RAMM *crosses to* DAN *in cot and shakes his shoulder*) Present ARMS. (*Sleepily*) What the...

RAMM

Stop that talking in your sleep. Very unorthodox. (DAN *looks at him. Pulls his hand from under the blanket and salutes sheepishly*) What's the matter, Crawford?

DAN

Sorry, sir, I had a terrible dream.

RAMM

Who's the room orderly? (*Goes to table.*)

DAN

Randolph, sir. (*Realizes too late he has made a fatal error.*)

RAMM

(*Glances toward other cots*)

This room is disgraceful. I've got a good mind to waken him and make him clean it up right away. (*Starts to cot in which* BILLY *is supposed to be sleeping.*)

DAN

(Scared, but thinking fast)

Sir, please. (COLONEL RAMM *stops*) He walked penalty tours, sir. He was awful tired. (COLONEL RAMM *thinks it over for a second or two, then looks toward* DAN.)

RAMM

Tell him to clean it up first thing in the morning.

DAN

Yes, sir.

RAMM

(Commands)

Go to sleep! (*Turns out lights.*)

DAN

Yes, sir. (COLONEL RAMM *exits*) Get the blankets up. All right?

BOTTOME

O.K. (BOTTOME *turns lights on.*)

CLAIRE

(Has been under the covers in the cot upstage. Out loud, as she emerges.)

"For thine is the kingdom and the power, and the glory, forever and ever. Amen." (*To* DAN) Is he gone?

DAN

Yeah, it's O.K. (*To* BOTTOME) Your knees are shaking, Mistol. Better sit down.

BOTTOME

Yes, sir. (BOTTOME *has been leaning against lockers and falls,*
with a sigh, into chair by door.)

DAN

You all right, Claire? (*Pulls rifle out from under covers.*)

CLAIRE

Old trusty. (*Pats rifle.*)

DAN

(*Goes to* CLAIRE, *and takes rifle*)

Here, give me that rifle. You'd better stick to chemistry. It's
safer. (*He replaces rifle in rack*) Wish you'd tell your old man
to stay away from our swinging doors. (CLAIRE *goes to back of*
table to help BING.)

CLAIRE

That's right, Bing. (*There is a knock heard on window.*
BING *puts light out, and general confusion reigns in dark.* BING
bangs knee against iron lockers and lets out loud wail. There
is not enough time to pull down blankets, and they all dive into
cots. A form enters through window.)

BILLY

(*In the dark, imitating voice of the Commandant*)

Very unorthodox, very unorthodox.

DAN

(*Recognizes* BILLY's *voice and turns on light*)

Nuts! You dim brain! (CLAIRE *is in cot left, her head buried*
in blankets. BILLY *stands there, laughing. He is dressed in a*
white paletot.)

181

BING

O.K., Mistol. (BOTTOME *crawls out from under cot and stag-gers to chair by door.*)

BILLY

(*Sees* CLAIRE)

Come outta the sand pile, Claire. You look like an ostrich.

CLAIRE

(*Sits up. Pulls head out of blankets. Looks up at* BILLY)

Hello, Billy. Have a good time?

BILLY

(*Sits on cot*)

Swell! (*To* DAN) Almost got snared, though.

DAN

How?

BILLY

Climbing in the window.

DAN

Commandant?

BILLY

No, the O.D.

DAN

(*Concerned*)

Did he see you?

BILLY

(*Over-confident*)

Hell, no.

182

CLAIRE
(*Slyly*)

A friend of yours was in here a minute ago. He was asking for you. (BOTTOME, *tired, has been slowly adjusting blanket, covering window.*)

BILLY

Yeah? Who was it?

BOTTOME
(*Yells*)

Jiggers! (*The door slams open.* HARRINGTON *in sash and sabre of O.D. storms into room.* BING *and* DAN *make a dash to pull out light. Both miss.* BING *is standing in ludicrous position, with* DAN *sitting on floor holding him up.* CLAIRE *is down on her knees between the two cots, with her "rear" sticking out.* DAN *crosses right on his hands and knees, then slowly comes to attention.*)

HARRINGTON

All right, Randolph, I saw you coming into barracks through that window. (*He spies* CLAIRE's *"rear"*) Well! Having a visitor? (*Short pause.* ALL *are speechless.*)

BING

Uh ... Mr. O.D. (*Pointing down at* CLAIRE) I know this looks sort of bad, but this girl ...

BILLY

Yes, Mr. O.D., we can explain the whole thing.

HARRINGTON

Don't bother. (*Gloating, he slowly paints the word picture*) Randolph, Crawford and Edwards ... All three of you under confinement... Caught with a woman in your room for immoral purposes... Dishonorably discharged a day before Commencement. (*He smiles smugly*) Sorry, gentlemen, but duty calls. I'm on my way to the Commandant. (*Turns and starts toward door.*)

CLAIRE
(*Rising*)

Mr. O.D.

HARRINGTON
(*Hears her voice and exclaims as he turns*)
What!

CLAIRE
(*As she turns toward him*)
Papa won't like it.

HARRINGTON
(*Recognizes her, takes a step back in amazement. Knowing he is stymied, he gasps*)
Migawd.

(*Blackout and curtain*)

ACT THREE

SCENE III

Nine P.M. The night before Commencement.
SCENE: *Barracks room, same as Act Three, Scene II.*
BILLY, ANDREWS *and* TOWNSEND *are grouped around the table,*
talking. TOWNSEND *and* BILLY *are wearing blouses and white*
trousers, ANDREWS *a paletot, and* DAN, *at shining stool, is wearing*
white pants and a sweater.

ANDREWS

So I wrote Sally to get ready for a real time.

TOWNSEND

That's exactly what I wrote my Gwendolyn.

ANDREWS

Can she read?

BILLY

Don't tell me you invited that pug-nosed red-head with the
four-word vocabulary down for finals.

TOWNSEND

You're darn right I did. And you wanna know something?

ANDREWS
(Artificial eagerness)
Yeah...

TOWNSEND

I'm gonna marry her.

BILLY
(*Can't believe it*)

Certify?

TOWNSEND
(*Firmly*)

Certify.

BILLY

If you marry that cipher-brain, Townsend, you'll have to spend the rest of your life drawing blue prints for her.

TOWNSEND
(*Piqued*)

She might not be brilliant, but she's an awful lot of fun.

ANDREWS

Yeah, how can you tell?

TOWNSEND

I've known her all my life.

DAN

Not a real childhood sweetheart?

TOWNSEND
(*As he sits*)

We didn't start as sweethearts. As a matter of fact, when I first knew her, we used to even fight, but then ... you know how two people get ... Well, you compromise ...

ANDREWS

How long did that take?

TOWNSEND

Oh, I don't know. We been sorta pals ... 'n' havin' fun since we were kids. We even used to climb trees together.

ANDREWS

Who went up first? (BING *enters. He is doleful-looking.*)

ANDREWS
(*Cheerfully*)

Hiya, Bing. The carbohydrates heard from yet?

BING
(*Doleful, crossing to sink, takes dipper of water*)

Naw.

TOWNSEND

What's a matter with Lace-Drawers? Isn't he ever goin' to post those grades?

BING
(*From sink*)

I figured out I got about a 71 on my daily average, so I've got to have over 80 in my final exam to pull me through.

TOWNSEND

Aw, Bing. That exam wasn't hard.

DAN

You said you worked all the problems.

BING

Yeah, I worked 'em. But did I work 'em right?

TOWNSEND

(*Rising*)

My roommate's Officer of the Guard. Maybe he's got some dope.

ANDREWS

(*Rises*)

Wait a minute, Tree-climber. I'll go with you. (ANDREWS *and* TOWNSEND *exit.*)

DAN

(*Quietly*)

What have you heard from the hospital, Bing?

BING

I called a half an hour ago.

BILLY

Approachin' the deadline?

BING

Not sure what they meant. That's why I'm scared.

DAN

What'd they say?

BING

Doin' as well as can be expected.

BILLY

Don't worry, Bing. Nothing in the world'll happen to Kate. It isn't in the books. (MR. BOTTOME *slides into the room and Finns-out.*)

188

DAN
(Loud, but good-naturedly)
What do you want, Mistol?

BOTTOME
Mr. Randolph told me to come down here tonight, sir.

BILLY
Oh, yeah. Anyone taken you in yet, Mistol? *(Crosses to radiator and takes broom.)*

BOTTOME
(Painfully)
Oh, yes, sir.

BILLY
(Stern)
Well, assume the angle, Mistol. (BOTTOME *bends over table, grasping ends with both hands.* BILLY *takes broom from corner, swings broom menacingly through air, and strikes* BOTTOME *on his buttocks with flat of broom. He then extends his hands to* BOTTOME) Call me Billy.

BOTTOME
(Happy to be his equal, smiles)
O.K., Billy.

DAN
(Points finger to spot at table. BOTTOME *"assumes angle."* DAN *takes broom, hits* BOTTOME. *Shakes his hand)*
Call me Dan.

BOTTOME
All right ... Dan.

BING
(Without looking at him)

Mister Bottome?

BOTTOME

Sir?

BING
(Sticks out hand)

Call me Bing.

BOTTOME
(Shaking his hand)

Thanks, Bing.

DAN

How does it feel to be an old cadet, Bottome?

BOTTOME

Did you ever see a robin's belly on the first day of spring?
(Rubs buttocks. A pause) Well ... *(Sheepishly)* So ... long ...
fellas. *(Starts toward door.)*

BILLY
(Catching BOTTOME *off guard. Shouts)*

Mistol! (BOTTOME, *forgetting he is an old cadet, and their
equal, Finns-out stiffly. Then, realizing his error, he relaxes. He
turns, wearing sheepish grin.)*

BOTTOME
(Good-naturedly)

Aw ... go to hell ... Randolph. *(They laugh, as* BOTTOME
exits. Whistles are heard off stage.)

190

DAN
(*Points to window*)

The girls.

BILLY
(*Jumps to feet and runs to window and beckons*)

Come here ... Hello, Joyce ... Hello, Claire. (*Girls appear in window.*)

JOYCE
(*From window. Agitated*)

I have to tell you something.

CLAIRE

How did you make out, Bing? Pass?

BING

Gee, I dunno ... Grades haven't been posted yet.

CLAIRE

Did I spot them right?

BING
(*Smiling*)

You sure did. (BING *crosses in front of table to girls.*)

JOYCE

Bing, come over here. We just came from the hospital.

BING
(*Jumping forward and crossing to window*)

Kate?

JOYCE

Yes.

BING

Gawd, Joyce ... anything ... happen yet? You know what I mean.

JOYCE

They wouldn't let us in to see her, but you better watch your step, Bing.

BING

What's the matter?

JOYCE

One of the nurses told us Lieutenant Rogers was there this afternoon.

BILLY

Lace Drawers?

BING
(*To* DAN)

Omigawd.

DAN

What'd he want?

JOYCE

Search me.

BILLY

Did he see her?

192

CLAIRE

We don't know. But we thought we'd better tell you.

BING
(*Thinking of consequences*)
Lace Drawers! God! (*Voice of* CORPORAL OF GUARD *heard outside window.*)

CORPORAL

Drive on away from that window. You, over there.

CLAIRE
(*Turning*)
O.K., Corporal. All will be quiet on the Western front.

JOYCE

Good-bye ... (*Withdraws from window.*)

DAN

'Bye.

BILLY

So long.

CLAIRE

'Bye. (*Disappears from window.* TOWNSEND *rushes in, all excited.*)

TOWNSEND

Hey, Bing. Hey, fellers. Listen, I know something.

DAN

What's a matter, Towse?

193

TOWNSEND

There's some chemistry grades on the desk in the Commandant's office.

BILLY

Did you see 'em?

TOWNSEND

No. Jackson saw a big envelope. It's marked "Chemistry."

BILLY

Is the door locked?

TOWNSEND
(*Excited*)

No.

BILLY

Well, I'll go in and get 'em ... (*He starts for door and* DAN *grabs his arm, restraining him.*)

DAN

Listen, Randolph. This is our last night. So for once in four years, let's just try and be normal.

BILLY

Aw, there's nothin' to it, Dan. We'll just take a quick gander at 'em, and we'll put 'em right back.

DAN
(*Turns, shaking head*)

I swear to Gawd ...

BILLY

Come on with me, Towse.

194

TOWNSEND

(*A little bit scared and backing up to lockers*)
Who, me?

BILLY

(*Gets cap and crosses to door*)
Sure. You gotta cover me while I go in. (*Exits, pushing*
TOWNSEND *ahead of him.* DAN *hurriedly crosses to door and
looks out, turns, sags against wall.*)

BING

(*Crossing to table, all confused*)
So many goddamned things are happenin'. I don't know
what I'm gonna do. Dan, do you think Lace Drawers knows
about Kate and me?

DAN

I don't know.

BING

If he does, I won't be needin' the grades.

DAN

Pull up your girdle, you'll know in a minute.

BING

(*Sits in chair*)
Gosh, Dan. I gotta graduate now.

DAN

You're darn right. And you've got to win that award.

BING

Yeah, but I gotta graduate first.

DAN

Gawd, this is tough on the ticker. (*Buries head in arms on table. Pause.*)

BING

(*Swallowing*)

Dan, d'you think prayin'd help any?

DAN

(*Looking up*)

What the hell do you think I'm doin'?

BING

I sorta wish Billy hadn't gone for the grades now.

DAN

(*Rises, nervously crosses to bookshelves*)

This is a swell time to think of it.

BING

I'd just as soon wait till tomorrow. (*Pause. Thinking back*) I worked all the problems.

DAN

(*Crossing to windows*)

Well, that's a step in the right direction.

BING

(*Still thinking back*)

I wonder if there was enough oxygen in that last equation. (BILLY *rushes in, waving a big manila envelope.*)

BILLY

Here they are. Read 'em and weep.

196

DAN

(*Rushes to table*)

Leapin' geez! You didn't bring 'em with you?

BILLY

(*Crossing to table*)

You don't think I was goin' to take a siesta in the Commandant's office? (*Pulls papers out of the envelope*) What's your section, Bing?

BING

Huh?

BILLY

(*Excited*)

Your section ... Step off ... I gotta get these back there.

BING

(*Excited, pounds on his head and finally stutters out answer*)

Five.

BILLY

(*Milling over papers in a hurry, as* DAN *looks over his left shoulder*)

Where the hell's five? Five ... Five ... (*As he thumbs them*) Here ... (*Looking through names*) Davis ... Eccles ... Edwards ...

DAN

What did he get? (*The bottom drops out as* BILLY *sees the grade is below passing.* BILLY *registers surprise and intense disappointment.* DAN *and* BING *know the result, from* BILLY'S *expression, and react with him. There is a dead pause.*)

197

BING
(*Quietly*)

Didn't ... I ... make it?

BILLY
(*Almost in tears*)

Geez ... Bing ... Seventy-three ... I'm sorry. (DAN *just look*
at BING. TOWNSEND *charges into room*.)

TOWNSEND
(*Agitated, bursts into room*)

Here comes Lace Drawers ...

BILLY

Ohmigawd ... Give me those papers. (*He starts picking them*
up and barely has time to collect them. Then he rushes to win-
dow and puts papers behind his back as LIEUTENANT "LACE
DRAWERS" ROGERS *enters.* ROGERS *is carrying confinement sheets*
and other papers. All snap to attention.)

ROGERS
(*Reading from paper*)

Crawford ... Randolph ... Edwards.

BILLY	DAN	BING
Yes, sir.	Yes, sir.	Yes, sir.

ROGERS

Having served a period of two months' confinement, expir-
ing tonight, you are hereby released, by order of the Commandant.

BILLY	DAN	BING
Yes, sir.	Yes, sir.	Yes, sir.

ROGERS

It was unfortunate that I was Officer in Charge at the time
our offense was committed, and it's rather satisfying that I'm
a duty the night your confinement expires.... Rest. Mr. Ed-
ards...

BING
(*Weakly*)

Sir?

ROGERS

That examination of yours... was a great surprise. (BING
reacts) The best bit of work you've handed in this year. How-
ver, it's a pity you got off on the wrong track in the last two
roblems. But I suppose 84 is a high enough mark for anyone.
nd since your daily grade is 73, as I recall it, you have passed
y a very comfortable margin. (*All three of the boys react joy-
usly and start looking at one another*) I'm going over to the
ommandant's office now to pick up the daily averages and
en I shall post the final results. Congratulations. You might
ass the word around that I'm posting the finals right away.
The boys are very much disturbed at this last report. ROGERS
osses to door, remembers something, returns to table*) Ed-
ards, I understand you know Miss Rice quite well.... (BING
ays.*)

BING

You mean... Kate Rice... sir?

ROGERS

That's right. (BILLY *and* DAN *freeze*) I was talking with her
other this afternoon... at the hospital in Staunton.

199

BING

(*Barely audible*)

Sir?

BILLY

(*Almost reverently*)

Is her mother ill ... sir?

ROGERS

No. Miss Rice is the one that's ill, and I understand her con dition is quite precarious.

BING

(*Vague*)

Sir?

BILLY

(*Slowly*)

Did you see her, sir?

ROGERS

No ... she's not allowed visitors. ... Must have absolute quie ... Nasty thing, appendicitis. (*At the word "Appendicitis," BIN falls in a heap on the floor. They all gather around BING an pull him into chair. DAN starts rubbing BING's head and BILL waves his cap at him.*)

DAN

(*Bending over him*)

Towse, get some water.

ROGERS

I guess the news about the grades was too much for him.

BILLY

Yes, sir.

DAN

(*Talking like a catcher*)
C'mon, C'mon, C'mon, Bing ol' boy. Give it to me in there.....
(TOWNSEND *brings a dipper of water.* BING *starts to come around and they give him a sip.*)

ROGERS

You all right, Edwards? (BING *looks up dazed*)

DAN

Oh, he'll be all right.

BILLY

He gets spells like this once in a while. I think it's his Vitamin D.

ROGERS

(*Starts to leave*)
Well, I hope he'll be all right....I suppose this is a rather crucial moment. Well, I must get along to the Commandant's office and pick up those grades. (*Crosses to door and* DAN *and* BILLY *nervously point to him.*)

TOWNSEND

(*Being smart for the first time in his life*)
Sir, may I ask a question of the Officer in Charge?

ROGERS
(*At door*)

Yes.

TOWNSEND

Sir ... uh ... I understand you're collecting some of the old chemistry books.

ROGERS

(*Crossing down to* TOWNSEND)

That's right.

TOWNSEND

Well, sir, ... I have a full set ... and ... if you'd like to have them for ... uh ... some cadet ... who ... uh ... couldn't afford them next year ...

ROGERS

Why, that's very nice of you, Townsend. (*Starts for door.*)

TOWNSEND

And ... uh ... if you want to ... You said you were going to the Commandant's office ... I'll be glad to just stop in my room with you on the way over and give them to you right now.

ROGERS

That'll be fine.

TOWNSEND

All right, sir. (*He lets* ROGERS *exit first.* TOWNSEND *comes back to chair near wash basin, picks up cap and starts for door.*)

BILLY

(*Sotto voce*)

Nice going, Towse.

TOWNSEND

(*Strutting to door. Stops and looks back*)

Townsend's the name ... Beaver Falls, P ... A ... (*Exits.*)

DAN
> (*To* BILLY)

Step off!

BILLY

I'll get there first. (*Exits quickly through window.*)

DAN
> (*Exuberantly*)

You pick out a swell time to fold up on us. Why don't you wear a sign?

BING
> (*Broad grin*)

Good news, eh? (*They joyously embrace each other.*)

DAN
> (*Shaking his head*)

You're a pip, you are...84!

BING
> (*Beaming*)

I'm gonna graduate. (*He crosses left, punching the air with his fists.*)

DAN

You sure are. It's been a long haul. (HARRINGTON *enters, dressed in white paletot.*)

DAN

Hello, Harley. Want to hear some good news?

HARRINGTON

Sure.

DAN

Bing knocked off an 84 in chemistry.

HARRINGTON

Eighty-four! Well...uh...How the hell did you ever do that?

BING

Well, you never know what you can do...till you have to.

HARRINGTON
(*Elated*)

I just got some good news, too.

DAN

What's that?

HARRINGTON

The Athletic Association just posted their selection.

BING
(*Eagerly*)

They did?

DAN
(*Anxiously*)

Who got it?

HARRINGTON
(*Trying to be modest*)

Well, Bing, you gave me quite a run for it. I guess it was pretty close.

DAN
(Shaking hands with HARRINGTON)
Congratulations, Harley.

HARRINGTON
Thanks. (DAN *turns away, obviously very sad about the new turn.*)

BING
Extending hand to HARRINGTON, *trying not to show disappointment*)
Well ... Harley ... that's great. I'm glad for you.

HARRINGTON
Thanks, Bing. See you later. (*Starts to exit, as* BILLY *enters.*)

BILLY
(As he enters)
Nothing to it. (*Looks at* HARRINGTON *for a second*) Hi, Harley, I heard the news. (*Shakes his hand, not too enthusiastically*) Great stuff.

HARRINGTON
Thanks. (*Exits.* BING *just sits. Nothing is said.* BILLY *crosses to* BING, *takes off cap, leans over table.*)

DAN
(Quietly)
To them that hath is given.

BILLY
(Straight, sincere and quietly)
Listen, Bing. It's just like a ten in a crap game. There's two ways to make it.... The easy way and the hard way—a six and

205

"BROTHER RAT"

a four or a pair of fives. (*Points toward door*) There's a gu
who all his life will make it the easy way. But, Brother Rat .
keep swingin'. You'll make it the hard way, and the pay off
seven to one. (MEMBER OF GUARD *enters, followed by* TOWNSEND

MEMBER OF GUARD

Edwards.

BILLY

Right here.

BING

Yeah?

MEMBER OF GUARD

Telegram for you.

BING

Huh? Thanks. (*Takes telegram.*)

BILLY

Where's it from?

BING

(*Opens telegram*)

Dunno. (MEMBER OF GUARD *exits. As* BING *reads telegram, hi.*
face lights up. All watch him expectantly. Almost screams as h
rises) Billy ... Dan ... A boy!

TOWNSEND

What?

DAN

I'll be goddamned!

206

BILLY
(Letting out a whoop)

Hoorayyyyyy!

BING
(Reading)
And Kate's all right.... Gee ... *(Screams)* A *boy!*

DAN
(Sardonically)
If he's anything like his old man, I feel sorry for his room-
mates.

BILLY
(Jumping around)
We ought to get drunk. We ought to get drunk.

TOWNSEND
For the love of mike, what is this?

DAN
(To TOWNSEND. *Turns him around)*
If you ever want to see Gwendolyn again, you'd better keep
your mouth shut until after tomorrow.

TOWNSEND
(Hurt)
Gosh, Dan... What d'yuh think I am? Don't you think I
got any ideals?

BILLY
He's all right. (DAN, *all excited over a new idea, crosses to*
window) We gotta have a name.... We gotta have a name....
It's a man without a country.

DAN

Hey, that's right. We gotta have a name.

TOWNSEND

Will you fellas please tell me ... *who's* got to have a name?

DAN

I've got it. Perfect! Commencement ... *Commencement!*

BILLY

(*Thinks it over quickly. Face lights up*)
Commencement ... Sure.... The time, the place, the hour.
Commencement Edwards it is. (*Crosses to* BING. *Sticking out his hand to* BING) Bing ... Congratulate us.... We've named your baby.

BING

(*Shaking his hand, beaming*)
Yeah, thanks ... *Commencement!*

BILLY

(*His face lights up with the most stupendous scoop he's ever made. As if an airplane had dropped into the room*)
Migawwwwwwd!

DAN

What's a matter?

BILLY

Lend me your ears to the most sensational development of all time!

ALL

What ... ?

208

BILLY

(*Points to* BING)

Brother Rat...You've won the baby prize. (*Shakes* BING's
and.)

DAN

Migawd, that's right. The first father in the class.

TOWNSEND

(*Whistling*)

Whew...Three hundred dollars!

BING

(*Screams with joy*)

Great day in the morning!

BILLY

(*Singing to the tune of "The Farmer in the Dell"*)

The baby's gonna eat.... The baby's gonna eat....

DAN

We've got to celebrate.

BILLY

(*Grabbing his cap*)

I've got to tell Joyce. (*Starts for window.*)

DAN

(*Crosses to locker, gets blouse. Enthusiastically*)

Wait a minute...I'm going with you.

BILLY

(*Starts toward window*)

Commencement Edwards...You can't even tie it.

209

TOWNSEND

Run the block ... Your last night?

BILLY

I'm migratory.

TOWNSEND

You're *nuts*.

BILLY

Nutty as a keechy bug. (DAN *jumps up to open section of window*.)

TOWNSEND

If you're caught, you'll get shipped.

DAN

If we get caught ... (DAN *jumps out of window*.)

BILLY

Dan'll have to marry the boss's daughter. (*Exits out window*.)

TOWNSEND

Migawd.

BING

(*Goes to window, looks out. Calls*)
Billy ... Dan ... Wait a minute. I'm going with you. (*Crosses to bookshelves, grabs cap, starts to window*.)

TOWNSEND

Bing ... You can't go.... You've got to graduate....

210

BING

(Running across room)

I've got to see Kate.

TOWNSEND

Migawd, Bing...Don't do it....Commencement is prac-cally here.

BING

(Smiles as he stands in window and waves telegram)
Practically, hell! He *is here.* (*Drops out of window, as the curtain falls.*)